walking with purpose

Dear Friend,

You are about to begin a journey that is going to engage your heart, broaden your mind, and change you from within. How can I make such a bold claim? It's because that's what Bible study consistently does. When we take in Scripture with our own eyes, wrestle with its truth as we study it at home, and then digest it through discussing it with others, the truths really start to take root and transform us.

We're told in Romans 12:2 that we're not to be conformed to our culture but are to be transformed by the renewal of our minds so that we can figure out what God's perfect will is. We live in a society that is highly individualistic. You are bombarded every day with countless messages saying that what really matters is your image, your profile, your platform, your comfort. God's perspective is a little different. He looks at your heart, and says *that is what matters most*.

God recognizes that our hearts are in need of some healing. He knows the answer isn't found in a trip to the spa, a glass of wine, or some retail therapy. God knows that the more our perspectives are filled with *Him*, the more all the things that wreck our hearts will fall into place. We'll see ourselves through His eyes. We'll see we are beloved. And the more we understand His greatness, His glory, His sovereignty, the more we'll appreciate what it means to be cherished by *Him*. The King of the Universe looks at you and says, "Chosen. Blessed. Treasured."

So how do we respond? May it be with a desire to know Him better. That's what *Beholding Your King* will help you to do. The Eternal One has revealed His character throughout Scripture. In this study, we'll discover Jesus, the Lamb of God, the King of kings, and the Lord of lords, in the pages of the Old Testament.

Love,

Lisa Brenninkmeyer
Founder and Chief Purpose Officer, Walking with Purpose

Beholding Your King
Christ Revealed in the Old Testament

Authored by Lisa Brenninkmeyer

Published by Walking with Purpose, Inc.

IMPRIMATUR   +William E. Lori, S.T.D., Archbishop of Baltimore

The recommended Bible translations for use in Walking with Purpose studies are: The New American Bible, which is the translation used in the United States for the readings at Mass; The Revised Standard Version, Catholic Edition; and The Jerusalem Bible.

Copyright © June 2010-2019 by Walking with Purpose, Inc.

All rights reserved. No part of this book may be reproduced in any form by any electronic or mechanical means (including photocopying, recording, or information storage and retrieval) without permission in writing from Walking with Purpose. Cover and page design by True Cotton.

Any internet addresses (websites, blogs, etc.) in this book are offered as a resource and may change in the future. Please refer to www.walkingwithpurpose.com as the central location for corresponding materials and references.

22 23 24 25 26 / 9 8 7 6 5 4 3

ISBN: 978-1-943173-06-8

Beholding Your King: Christ Revealed in the Old Testament
(RSV)

Printed in the United States of America

TABLE OF CONTENTS

INTRODUCTION
Welcome to Walking with Purpose 3
The Structure of *Beholding Your King* 3
Study Guide Format and Reference Materials 4
Walking with Purpose™ Website 5

LESSONS
Overview of Salvation History 9
1 Connect Coffee Talk 1: The Shepherd King – I Lead You with Care 15
2 David 19
3 Psalm 23 41
4 A Medley of Psalms 59
5 Connect Coffee Talk 2: The Temple – I Invite You In 77
6 Isaiah 53 81
7 Jeremiah and Ezekiel 99
8 The Throne Room 117
9 Connect Coffee Talk 3: Jesus – I'm Deserving of Worship 133

APPENDICES
1 Saint Thérèse of Lisieux 139
2 Scripture Memory 141
    Memory Verse Card: Phillipians 3:19 145
3 How to Do a Verse Study 147
4 Covenants – God's Family Bond 151
5 Conversion of Heart 155
6 Litany of Praise 159

ANSWER KEY 161

PRAYER PAGES 183

NOTES

Welcome to Walking with Purpose

You have many choices when it comes to how you spend your time—thank you for choosing Walking with Purpose. Studying God's Word with an open and receptive heart will bring spiritual growth and enrichment to all aspects of your life, making every moment that you've invested well worth it.

Each one of us comes to this material from our own unique vantage point. You are welcome as you are. No previous experience is necessary. Some of you will find that the questions in this study cause you to think about concepts that are new to you. Others might find much is a review. God meets each one of us where we are, and He is always faithful, taking us to a deeper, better place spiritually, regardless of where we begin.

The Structure of *Beholding Your King*

Beholding Your King is a nine-session Bible study that integrates Scripture with the teachings of the Roman Catholic Church, showing us how all Scripture points us to our Redeemer, Jesus Christ. As we look at Old Testament people and events, we'll encounter problems that only Christ will solve, needs that only He will satisfy, and promises that only He can deliver on.

Beholding Your King is designed for both interactive personal study and group discussion.

If you are going through *Beholding Your King* with a small group in your parish, most weeks will be spent in the small group discussing one of the lessons from the *Beholding Your King Study Guide*. Three of the lessons provide the opportunity to gather for a Connect Coffee, which consists of social time, a DVD presentation of one of the related Bible study talks, and small group discussion of selected questions that relate to the talk.

If you're going through this study either on your own or in a small group, you are welcome to order the DVDs, but you might find it simpler to watch the talks online.

The URL for each talk is listed on the Connect Coffee Talk outline within the study guide.

Study Guide Format and Reference Materials

The *Beholding Your King Study Guide* is divided into three sections:

The first section comprises nine lessons. Most lessons are divided into five "days" to help you form a habit of reading and reflecting on God's Word regularly. If you are a woman who has only bits and pieces of time throughout your day to accomplish tasks, you will find this breakdown of the lessons especially helpful. Each day focuses on Scripture readings and related teaching passages, and ends with a Quiet Your Heart reflection. In addition, Day Five includes a lesson conclusion; a resolution section, in which you set a goal for yourself based on a theme of the lesson; and short clips from the *Catechism of the Catholic Church*, which are referenced throughout the lesson to complement the Scripture study. Each lesson ends with a relevant verse study. Instructions for how to do a verse study can be found in Appendix 3.

For the Connect Coffee Talks in the series, accompanying outlines are offered as guides for taking notes. Included are questions to help direct your group's discussion following the talks, as well as URLs for those who would like to view the talks online.

The second section, the appendices, contains supplemental materials referred to during the study, and includes an article about Saint Thérèse of Lisieux, the patron saint of Walking with Purpose (Appendix 1). Appendix 2, "Scripture Memory," gives instructions on how to memorize Scripture. One memory verse has been chosen for *Beholding Your King*, and we encourage you to memorize it as you move through the Bible study. An illustration of the verse can be found at the back of the study guide, and a color version and phone lock screen can be downloaded from our website.

The third section contains the answer key. You will benefit so much more from the Bible study if you work through the questions on your own, searching your heart, as this is your very personal journey of faith. The answer key is meant to enhance small group discussion, and provide personal guidance or insight when needed.

At the end of the book are pages on which to write weekly prayer intentions.

Walking with Purpose™ Website

Please visit our website at www.walkingwithpurpose.com to find additional free content, supplemental materials that compliment our Bible studies, as well as a link to our online store for additional Bible studies, DVDs, book and more!

WWP Scripture Printables of our exclusively designed verse cards that compliment all Bible studies. Available in various sizes, lock screens for phones, and a format that allows you to e-mail them to a friend.

WWP Bible Study Playlists of Lisa's favorite music accompany each Bible study.

WWP Videos of all Connect Coffee Talks by Lisa Brenninkmeyer.

WWP Blog by Lisa Brenninkmeyer you are welcome to come here to find a safe place where the mask can drop and you can be real. Subscribe for updates.

WWP Leadership Development Program
We are here to help you take your leadership to the next level! Through our training, you'll discover insights that help you achieve your leadership potential. You'll be empowered to step out of your comfort zone and experience the rush of serving God with passion and purpose. We want you to know that you are not alone; we offer you encouragement and the tools you need to reach out to a world that desperately needs to experience the love of God.

Links to WWP Social Media

Twitter, Pinterest, Facebook, Instagram

Lessons

NOTES

Walking with Purpose is a community of women growing in faith – together! This is where women are gathering. Join us!

www.walkingwithpurpose.com

Overview of Salvation History

The way that most of us understand the Bible has come from hearing each of its stories separately. Often, we look at an individual person or event and try to see what we're supposed to learn. While "all Scripture is inspired by God and profitable for teaching, for reproof, for correction, and for training in righteousness" (2 Timothy 3:16), we do the Bible a disservice when we fail to grasp the overall big picture and core message.

Looking at the Bible as a whole, we see that it's one continuous story of mankind's need for love, forgiveness, redemption, and completion. It reveals God's plan to rescue mankind—a plan set in place at the very beginning—and the way in which Jesus ultimately makes everything new and right. This is what we're going to explore in *Beholding Your King*. We will be looking at individual people, places, and events, but instead of studying them only in the Old Testament context, we'll discover in each one of them a glimpse of the coming Savior.

The first promise of a rescuer came in the Garden of Eden, directly following the entrance of sin into the world. God told **Adam and Eve** there would be consequences for choosing their way over His way. He revealed to Adam that work would always be hard, Eve's childbearing would be painful, and their most important relationships would be marred by sin. The serpent who had tempted them to sin received his own curse. God said that there would be "enmity between [the serpent] and the woman [Mary], and between [his] seed and her seed; he shall bruise [the serpent's] head, and [the serpent] shall bruise his heel" (Genesis 3:15). This verse is referred to as the protoevangelium, or the first glimpse of the gospel. God didn't say that sin doesn't matter. God didn't say that sin doesn't have consequences. But God did say that sin doesn't have the last word. Nor did God promise that mankind would someday be perfect. He just promised that one day, a perfect One would come.

Adam and Eve were expelled from the Garden of Eden, and went on to have children. Their children's children began to fill the earth. Unfortunately, they followed in their parents' footsteps, choosing what they felt like choosing, and doing what seemed right at the time. Their choices were not the ones God had asked them to make. When God looked at mankind, it broke His heart. By choosing their own way, His people were rejecting Him. God saw one man amid the mess who was standing his ground in the midst of a wicked culture. This man was **Noah**. God decided to wipe out the evil in the world through a flood, but to save Noah and his family in the ark. Outside, everyone perished. When the ark came to rest on dry ground, Noah and his family made a fresh start. But even though Noah had been righteous, he wasn't perfect. Evil and sin wasn't something "out there." Even though he could point to countless people who were worse than he was, the dividing line between good and bad didn't run along the threshold of the ark. It ran down the middle of every person's heart. Sinful men stepped into the ark, were saved by grace, and stepped out, still prone to making the wrong choices. They still needed a rescue.

As Noah's descendants grew in number, they also began to advance in terms of skill. They wanted to build a tower that would bring glory to themselves instead of God. Since God created man to "know Him, to love Him, and to serve Him in this world, and to be happy with Him for ever in heaven,"[1] their plan wasn't going to bring them to a place of true fulfillment. So God confused their language at the **Tower of Babel**, preventing them from settling for a counterfeit version of fulfillment, and the people were scattered over the whole earth.

Years went by, and people continued to muddle along, always struggling with the same issues that had faced their ancestors. God chose one man, **Abraham**, to bless in a special way. He promised Abraham that he would not only have a son (his greatest dream), but that he would become a great nation that would bless the whole world. That promised son was Isaac, and his life pointed to the ultimate promised One, who would be one of Abraham's descendants many hundreds of years later. This promised One would bless the whole earth through His sacrificial love and gift of life.

Isaac had two sons, Jacob and Esau. God had told Isaac that the promised blessing was to go through Jacob's line, not Esau's. But Esau was Isaac's favorite son. Isaac had every intention of doing things his way and giving the blessing to Esau instead of Jacob, but Jacob dressed up as his brother and tricked his blind father into giving him the blessing instead. As a result of his deception, he had to flee, and never saw his father or mother again.

Jacob had twelve sons from two wives and two servants. Although the beginning of his story was one of treachery, after wrestling with God, Jacob was given a new start and a new name, Israel. Israel's twelve sons became the twelve tribes of Israel. Just as his father had before him, Israel had a favorite child. His favorite son was **Joseph**, and he did nothing to hide this. Jealousy among the other sons resulted, and in anger, they sold Joseph into slavery in Egypt. Proving that God can turn curses into blessings, Joseph became the most powerful man in Egypt next to the Pharaoh. He saved his entire family from starvation during the famine. Israel and his sons and all their families moved to Egypt and flourished there.

Years passed, and the new Pharaoh didn't remember Joseph. He was threatened by the Israelites, because there were simply so many of them. Enslaving them seemed the

---

[1] Baltimore Catechism 1, question 6.

best way to keep them under control, and for hundreds of years they languished in Egypt. God raised up a rescuer for them—an Israelite who, by God's provision, had been raised by Pharaoh's daughter. Through **Moses**, God performed miracles and wonders that no one had ever seen before. The Israelites were led out of Egypt, and God began to prepare them to be free people, His chosen nation.

Under the leadership of **Joshua**, the Israelites conquered Canaan, and the Promised Land became their home. For years, they were led by judges, who were raised up at key points in the Israelites' history to bring the people victory from oppressors. Judges were their human leaders, but the One truly leading and protecting Israel was God Himself.

It wasn't long before the Israelites started comparing themselves to the surrounding nations, wanting to be just like them. They wanted a human king. God gave them what they wanted, first with King Saul, then King **David**, then King Solomon. King David had a heart for the Lord, and God promised him that one of his descendants would always be on the throne. The throne was passed to his son, Solomon, who started well. Under Solomon's reign, **the Temple** in Jerusalem was built, and the Israelite people enjoyed a period of peace. Solomon grew very wealthy, and his palace and riches were admired by all. But the opulence and majesty of all he had came at a price. The Israelite people had been taxed and burdened by all the building. By the time King Solomon was passing the crown to his son, Rehoboam, the people were weary.

Rehoboam asked two groups of advisers how he should respond to the people as their new ruler. He first asked the older advisers, who had served his father. They recommended that Rehoboam give the people a break because they had already given so much. Rehoboam then asked his friends, the young men who were set to rule alongside him. They recommended that he show the people his strength by demanding even more. Rehoboam listened to his friends, and as a result, the people rebelled and the nation split in two, becoming the Divided Kingdom.

The Northern Kingdom, now known as Israel, was ruled by Jeroboam. The Southern Kingdom, now called Judah, was ruled by Rehoboam. Jeroboam had more of the tribes on his side, but Rehoboam had Jerusalem within his borders. Jeroboam didn't want his people traveling to the temple to worship, because he feared they would no longer be loyal to him. So Jeroboam set up his own places of worship, in direct defiance of God. The nation of Israel fell into idolatry and completely rejected God. Judah wasn't much better. While there were examples of holy kings in the Southern Kingdom's history, overall, they, too, were characterized by disobedience and rebellion against God.

God raised up prophets to speak to both Israel and Judah, encouraging them to turn back to Him. The prophets Hosea and **Isaiah** were contemporaries. Hosea was sent to the Northern Kingdom (Israel) and Isaiah was sent to the Southern Kingdom (Judah), in hopes that both kingdoms would return to God wholeheartedly.

To understand what happened next, it's helpful to look back to the renewal of the covenant that took place at the end of Moses' ministry. Before his death, Moses had set before Israel two choices: They could obey the covenant, which would bring God's blessings upon the people; or they could disobey, which would bring curses upon the people. Moses said:

> See, I have set before you this day life and good, death and evil. If you obey the commandments of the Lord your God, which I command you this day, by loving the Lord your God, by walking in his ways, and by keeping his commandments and his statutes and his ordinances, then you shall live and multiply and the Lord your God, will bless you in the land which you are entering to take possession of it [the Promised Land]. But if your heart turns away, and you will not hear, but are drawn away to worship other gods and serve them, I declare to you this day, that you shall perish; you shall not live long in the land which you are going over the Jordan to enter and possess. I call heaven and earth to witness against you this day, that I have set before you life and death, blessing and curse; therefore choose life, that you and your descendants may live, loving the Lord your God, obeying his voice, and clinging to him; for that means life for you and length of days, that you may dwell in the land which the Lord swore to your fathers, to Abraham, to Isaac, and to Jacob, to give them. (Deuteronomy 30:15–20)

The Northern Kingdom's rebellion against God brought down curses in 722 BC, during Isaiah's ministry to the Southern Kingdom. God allowed the nation of Assyria to conquer them, in fulfillment of Deuteronomy 30. The Assyrians invaded and took most of the people of the Northern Kingdom out of their land, just as God had said. The Israelites were scattered. In their place, "the king of Assyria brought people from Babylon, Cuthah, Avva, Hamath, and Sepharvaim, and placed them in the cities of Samaria instead of the sons of Israel" (2 Kings 17:24). Five nations resettled in what had been the Promised Land. The remaining Israelites intermarried with these nations, and with time they utterly assimilated into this mixed culture. These people were called the Samaritans during the time of Christ.

When Isaiah was preaching to the Southern Kingdom, what had happened in the north should have served as a reminder that infidelity has consequences. Some in the south took heed of Isaiah's words. Too many did not.

Although Isaiah spent his life pleading with the people in the Southern Kingdom of Judah to turn from sin and obey God, they chose to disobey. As a result, God allowed them to be conquered by Babylon. The Israelites in the Southern Kingdom were deported from the Promised Land in three stages. During the first, the best and brightest in the kingdom were taken to King Nebuchadnezzar in Babylon to work for him. **Daniel** was one of these men. The second deportation was the largest. Jerusalem was captured and ten thousand Jews were deported. The prophet and priest **Ezekiel** was in the second deportation, and his words ministered greatly to the exiles. The third deportation saw the execution of members of the royal family and officials. Jerusalem was destroyed. The prophet **Jeremiah** prophesied during all three exiles. "The influence of Jeremiah was greater after his death than before. The exiled community read and meditated on the lessons of the prophet; his influence is evident in Ezekiel, some of the psalms, Is. 40–66 and Daniel."[2] Jeremiah was eventually exiled to Egypt and the details of his death remain unknown.

The Jewish people in Babylon were allowed to return and rebuild Jerusalem and the temple during the rule of Cyrus of Persia. Following that period of history, the Jewish people were ruled by the Greeks. The books 1 and 2 Maccabees tell of their revolt against the Greeks, who tried to force the Jewish people to worship idols.

God's children were home, but they weren't free. They still longed for a rescuer, for a deliverer. A spirit of expectancy grew among the people. When would the Messiah come? When would God fulfill His promise? Who would be the mother of this special child? And because God *always* keeps His promises, *always* is faithful and true, **Jesus** came. He came to deliver the Jewish people, He came to forgive and redeem His enemies, He came to bring freedom to you and me.

---

[2] Introduction to "The Book of Jeremiah," Life Teen Bible (Mesa, AZ: Life Teen, 2009), 912.

Lesson 1: Connect Coffee Talk

THE SHEPHERD KING – I LEAD YOU WITH CARE

Accompanying talk can be viewed by DVD or digital download purchase or access online at walkingwithpurpose.com/videos.

1. The Characteristics of the Good Shepherd

   A. He promises to lay down His life for us.

      John 10:11–13

   B. He promises to know and guide us.

      John 10:27

      Jeremiah 1:5

      Luke 12:7

      Psalm 139

C. He promises to sustain us and carry us when we are weak.

   Isaiah 40:11

   Ezekiel 34:16

2. **The Right Response for the Sheep**

   Psalm 91:1–3

   Psalm 59:9–10

   1 John 4:4

   1 Peter 5:8

   Matthew 10:22

Questions for Discussion

1. Have you struggled with the thought that you are never enough? In what area of life? Does this experience of "scarcity" cause you to want to just give up, or does it encourage you to turn up the pressure and strive to be more?

2. One of the characteristics of our Good Shepherd, Jesus, is that He keeps all His promises. In the talk, we looked at His promise to lay down His life for us, to know and guide us, to sustain and carry us when we are weak. Which of these three promises means the most to you right now?

3. Is there something you fear at this moment? Can you think of a characteristic of God that points to His sufficiency for you during this time when you feel afraid? Do you know someone who has "faithfully given himself or herself over to the goodness of God"—trusting God in the face of difficult circumstances? Share his or her story.

NOTES

Looking for more material? We've got you covered! Walking with Purpose meets women where they are in their spiritual journey. From our Opening Your Heart 22-lesson foundational Bible study to more advanced studies, we have something to help each and every woman grow closer to Christ. Find out more:

www.walkingwithpurpose.com

Lesson 2

DAVID

Introduction

It amazed me the number of times that William could fall down in one day. He was learning to walk, and countless times he'd take a tumble, only to lift his little rear up in the air again and set off with a determined, if wobbly, gait. There would be a few tears when he fell, but after a hug, he'd get right back up and try again.

If only the same could be said for me. I can remember a morning when I was busy getting William ready for the day. I was heavily pregnant with our fourth child, and the doorbell began to ring. I could hear its chime over and over again, and became progressively irritated that no one else in the house was going and answering it. "It's always up to me," I muttered under my breath. With as much fanfare as I could muster (I am a *very* good martyr), I ran to the door. Big mistake. I slipped on something wet, and up went my feet, and down came my head, full force, on the marble floor. Unlike William, I did *not* lift my not-so-little rear up in the air again to set off with a determined gait.

Why is it so much harder for adults to fall? They are falling from a far greater height than a child.

Perhaps this is why Jesus wants us to have a childlike faith. When we approach the spiritual life with the humility of a child, our falls don't take us by surprise. And when they occur, we run immediately into our Father's arms, begging Him for His kiss of mercy.

Childlike faith isn't full of pride. Pride can be very subtle. It often is hidden in the heart of a person who becomes extremely discouraged after falling into sin. Some people mistakenly consider statements like "How could I? I'm a horrible person! I'm worthless!" to be based in humility, but they are actually pride based. They come out of a heart that is surprised by its own weakness.

David's achievements scaled the heights, and his failures plumbed the depths. Throughout his life, the one constant was his return to his heavenly Father. He wasn't perfect, and he had a long list of falls after his name. Countless times in his life, self-reflection would lead him to the conclusion that he had become what he never wished to be. But instead of responding to that truth with self-pity, he turned to God, trusting that His mercy would be enough to cleanse him.

"God opposes the proud, but gives grace to the humble" (1 Peter 5:5). God has the heart of a father. Our Father cannot resist when His child stretches out her arms, asking Him to pick her up and set her back on the path to holiness. In the depths of his heart, David believed that God was this kind of Father, and it made all the difference.

Day One
A MAN AFTER GOD'S OWN HEART

Read 1 Samuel 16:1–13.

At the start of this passage, the prophet Samuel was grieving for Saul, the King of Israel. Saul's kingship had started with so much potential for good. He had been "a handsome young man. There was not a man among the sons of Israel more handsome than he; from his shoulders upward he was taller than any of the people" (1 Samuel 9:2). When Samuel had presented him to the Israelite people, he had said, "Do you see him whom the Lord has chosen? There is none like him among all the people" (1 Samuel 10:24). If Saul would have obeyed God and listened to His voice, then God would have remained with him, bringing blessing and protection. But Saul's downfall was his disregard for God's commands. It wasn't that he completely ignored what God had said. He just settled for partial obedience. This wasn't what God required, and so He rejected Saul as king. The spirit of the Lord departed from him.

1. Whom did Samuel think God would choose as the next king, and why? What was God's response to Samuel's assumption?

David | 2

2. What do Psalm 78:70–72 and Acts 13:22 reveal about the heart of David? What was it about his heart that caused God to choose him instead of Saul?

3. Out of all the boys in David's family, he was an unlikely choice for king. How do we know this? When Samuel told David's father, Jesse, to gather his sons together, he didn't even bother to send for David. Samuel had to ask him, "Are all your sons here?" How was Jesse's impression of David similar to the way many people looked at Jesus? Read the prophet Isaiah's description of Jesus in Isaiah 53:2–3 and the Jewish people's response to His coming in John 1:11.

4. What was David's occupation when God chose to anoint him as Israel's next king? How does this point to Christ? See 1 Samuel 16:11 and 17:34–35, and John 10:14–15.

5. David's life has many examples of both his heroic obedience to God and his disappointing choices that carried enormous consequences. David killed the great Philistine Goliath with nothing but a sling and a stone because he knew that victory came from God's hands and God could use anyone and anything. David loved his people and protected them. He loved God's law, as seen through his writings in the Psalms. But he also fell, and fell hard. He had an affair with Bathsheba, and then had her husband killed to cover his tracks. He failed in the area of parenting, allowing his sons to behave in ways that destroyed his family. How is it possible that David was a man after God's own heart? To answer, read the following verses, noting the qualities in David that caused God to respond very differently to him than He had responded to Saul.

2 Samuel 6:14–15, 20–22 (a description of David as he brought the Ark of God to Bethlehem): "And David danced before the Lord with all his might; and David was belted with a linen ephod. So David and all the house of Israel brought up the ark of the Lord with shouting, and with the sound of the horn. . . . And David returned to bless his household. But Michal the daughter of Saul came out to meet

David, and said, 'How the king of Israel honored himself today, uncovering himself today the eyes of his servants' maids, as one of the vulgar fellows shamelessly uncovers himself!' And David said to Michal: 'It was before the Lord, who chose me above your father, and above all his house, to appoint me as prince over Israel, the people of the Lord—I will make merry before the Lord. I will make myself more contemptible that this, and I will be abased in your eyes; but by the maids of whom you have spoken, by them I shall be held in honor.'"

Psalm 51:1–3 (written by David after his sin with Bathsheba): "Have mercy on me, O God, according to your merciful love; according to your abundant mercy blot out my transgressions. Wash me thoroughly from my iniquity, and cleanse me from my sin! For I know my transgressions, and my sin is ever before me."

1 Chronicles 29:11, 14 (David's prayer before he passed the kingship to his son Solomon): "Yours, O Lord, is the greatness, and the power, and the glory, and the victory, and the majesty; for all that is in the heavens and in the earth is yours; yours is the kingdom, O Lord, and you are exalted as head above all. . . . But who am I, and what is my people, that we should be able thus to offer willingly? For all things come from your, and of your own have we given you."

Quiet your heart and enjoy His presence. . . . While man looks at outward appearance, the Lord gazes on your heart.

Do you long to be a woman after God's own heart? Do you sometimes get discouraged when you see the chasm between how you behave and how you would like to be? Can you relate to what Saint Thérèse of Lisieux said about there being such a difference between her level of holiness and the holiness of the saints that she could compare it to "a mountain whose summit is lost in the heavens and an obscure grain of sand, trampled under the feet of passersby"?

Don't be discouraged. God recognizes our weakness, and realizes that perfection is a lofty goal for little children. "The eyes of the Lord roam over the whole earth, to encourage those who are devoted to him wholeheartedly," (2 Chronicles 16:9 NAB). What is God searching for? He is looking for a devoted heart.

Take some time to talk to God about your desire to have a heart like His. Admit your weakness, and ask Him to fulfill in your life the promise He made in 2 Corinthians 12:9: "My grace is sufficient for you, for my power is made perfect in weakness." Jesus will do for us what we cannot. What is lacking in our hearts is present in His. He will take our sin and give us His righteousness. He will fill our hearts with His own virtues. When we ask Him, He will come into our lives and fill in the gap. Yes, we are weak. Yes, we will fail and fall short. But if we ask Him, Jesus will make up for what we do badly and leave undone. His heart is fully devoted to us, and it knows us intimately. Don't try to go through life in your own strength when Jesus is just waiting to give you His.

Day Two
A SAFE PLACE TO GO DEEP

The readings today highlight David's relationship with King Saul's son Jonathan. Theirs was an unusual relationship, a rare bond of selfless friendship. "When he has finished speaking to Saul, the soul of Jonathan was knit to the soul of David, and Jonathan loved him as his own soul" (1 Samuel 18:1). Jonathan and David entered into a bond of friendship, and to signify his seriousness about this commitment, "Jonathan made a covenant with David, because he loved him as his own soul. And Jonathan stripped himself of the robe that was upon him, and gave it to David, and his armor, and even his sword and his bow and his belt" (1 Samuel 18:3–4).

The greatest obstacle to their friendship was the anger and jealousy that Saul felt toward David. When David returned from killing Goliath, the women in the streets came out to meet Saul and sang, "Saul has slain his thousands, and David his ten thousands" (1 Samuel 18:7). Saul became possessed by an evil spirit, and his rage for David knew no limit. Jonathan would have to decide where to place his loyalty.

Read 1 Samuel 20.

1. What was the personal cost to Jonathan when he chose to be loyal to David instead of Saul? What did it reveal about his character? See 1 Samuel 20:31.

2. Have you ever experienced the rare gift of a true friendship like the one between David and Jonathan, one in which each of you truly wants the best and is willing to make sacrifices for the other? Describe that friendship and what makes it so special.

David and Jesus had different levels of intimacy in terms of their relationships with people. There was an outer circle of people they interacted with, then a group of people who were closer, and finally the small circle of people with whom they were most intimate. David had a band of followers who were drawn to his charismatic leadership. He offered them a sense of belonging, purpose, and protection. He served them as a faithful leader, and they in turn offered their loyalty.[3] Jesus was followed by a multitude of people with illnesses and other needs. They were drawn to Him because He offered them healing and hope.[4] His love drew one person after another to His side. These were the people David and Jesus led and taught in a large group setting. While the individual relationships weren't intimate, they were significant because lives were changed as a result of their interactions.

David also led a smaller group of trusted individuals known as his officials. They had more contact with him than the average Israelite and were a part of the inner workings of his kingdom.[5] Jesus had His relationship with the twelve disciples.[6] Those relationships were ones that Jesus and David poured into, offering both service and leadership.

---

[3] 1 Samuel 22:1–2: "David departed from there and escaped to the cave of Adul′lam; and when his brothers and all his father's house heard it, they went down there to him. And every one who was in debt, and every one was discontented, gathered to him; and he became captain over them. And there were with him about four hundred men."

[4] Matthew 14:13–14: "Now when Jesus heard this, he withdrew from there in a boat to a lonely place apart. But when the crowds heard it, they followed him on foot from the towns. As he went ashore he saw a great throng; and his had compassion on them, and healed their sick."

[5] 2 Samuel 8:15–18: "So David reigned over all Israel; and David administered justice and equality to all his people. Jo′ab the son of Zeru′iah, was over the army; and Jehosh′aphat the son of Ahi′lud was recorder; and Zad′ok the son of Ahi′tub and Ahim′elech the son of Abi′athar were priests; and Serai′ah was secretary; and Bena′iah the son of Jehoi′ada was over the Cher′ethites and the Pel′ethites; and David's sons were priests."

[6] Matthew 10:2–4: "The names of the twelve apostles are these: first, Simon, who is called Peter, and Andrew his brother; James the son of Zeb′edee, and John his brother; Philip and Bartholomew; Thomas and Matthew the tax collector; James the son of Alphae′us, and Thaddae′us; Simon the Cananean, and Judas Iscariot, who betrayed him."

3. Both David and Jesus had an inner circle. These were the friends who were allowed to see more of their private lives than others. Certainly Jonathan was one of these friends for David. Who were the closest friends of Jesus? How would you describe the relationships they experienced with those in the "inner circle"? See Mark 5:37 and Matthew 17:1–2 and 26:36–37.

4. Both David and Jesus had times in their lives when they entered a place of grief so intense that no friend could accompany them there. The multitudes were gone, the officials and disciples were missing, and the inner circle of friends could only come so far. When did this occur in David's life? When did it occur in Jesus' life? What were friends able to do for them at this time? Were David and Jesus truly alone? See Psalm 3 and Matthew 26:38–39.

Quiet your heart and enjoy His presence. . . . He enters the deepest part of us, the place reserved for God alone.

We, like David and Jesus, have varied levels of intimacy in our relationships. There are the people we interact with day to day. Ideally, our presence in their lives is a blessing as God's love flows between us. There are other people with whom we go deeper. We're more intentional about our relationships with them. We give a little more of ourselves, and expect more in return. Then there is the small circle of people with whom we really share our hearts. These sacred friendships are incredibly important, and we should choose them wisely. When we open our hearts in this way, it should be to people who will encourage us to live in the way that God wants us to live. There's tremendous potential for influence—good and bad—in the inner circle. The transparency there should ideally create an atmosphere of loving accountability.

There comes a time in each of our lives when we must encounter circumstances unaccompanied by an earthly friend. Perhaps it's in the depths of grief, or in the midst of pain that we cannot share, or as we face serious illness. This is the place where the most serious decisions are made. We, like Jesus, go on our faces before God, and honestly wrestle with His will. What will be decided in that place? Will we surrender to Him? Will we trust Him? Will we be satisfied with Him? Will we allow Him to have His way in our lives, even if it means the circumstances aren't the ones we want? We do not enter that place alone. There is a friend who sticks closer than a brother. That friend is Jesus. There is nothing we experience that He does not understand.

"For we have not a high priest who is unable to sympathize with our weaknesses, but one who is every respect has been tempted as we are, yet without sinning. Let us then with confidence draw near to the throne of grace, that we may receive mercy and find grace to help in time of need" (Hebrews 4:15–16).

Day Three
LOVING YOUR ENEMIES

Read 2 Samuel 1.

1. How did David respond to the news of the deaths of Saul and Jonathan?

2. It isn't a surprise that David deeply mourned the loss of his dear friend Jonathan. The response that was unusual was his reaction to *Saul's* death. What did David say about Saul in his eulogy, found in 2 Samuel 1:19–27?

Note: Some people have interpreted 2 Samuel 1:26 as a reference to a homosexual relationship between David and Jonathan. This is an incorrect interpretation of this verse. There are many other places in Scripture where homosexuality is referred to[7] and this is not one of them. David and Jonathan were soul mates—best friends. Their love was *philios*, a holy friendship. What David had experienced in his friendship with Jonathan was unusual, something he possibly never experienced with a woman. He experienced Jonathan making an incredible sacrifice for him when Jonathan did all he

---
[7] Leviticus 18:22, 20:13; Romans 1:24–27; 1 Corinthians 6:9–10; 1 Timothy 1:10; Jude 7.

could to ensure that David could be king—a position that Jonathan should have inherited. This was a "wondrous" sacrifice. There was nothing sexual in their relationship. Many people respond to this by saying that we can interpret all of these Scriptures differently, and as we choose. While God does teach us in very personal ways as we read the Scriptures, as Catholics, we defer to those with the competence to teach and interpret. The magisterium (the teaching office of the Catholic Church) is a gift given to us by the Church, helping us to understand the Bible in light of its context and true intent. The magisterium doesn't stand in authority over the Bible, but it does guide its interpretation and give moral guidance. The purpose of the magisterium's guidance is *not* to prevent us from reading the Bible on our own and gaining insight. Its purpose is to prevent confusion, misinterpretation, and compromise. See CCC 85 and 86 for further insight.

3. In light of King Saul's long quest to kill David, it was astounding that David could speak of him so kindly. He was able to do this because he had truly forgiven Saul. That forgiveness had brought him to a place of being able to love his enemy. We may not have dealt with someone plotting our death, but it doesn't have to be something as serious as that to make it hard for us to forgive. When we've been wronged by someone, why should we forgive? See Mark 11:25 and 10:8.

4. How did Jesus respond when He was insulted and suffered? Why was He able to respond in this way? What can we learn from His example? See 1 Peter 2:23.

Quiet your heart and enjoy His presence. . . . He can be trusted to judge justly.

It's very difficult to hand over to God the right to judge a person who has really hurt us. That being said, the bigger view we have of Him, the easier it will be. If we have a small view of God, we're not going to be as likely to trust His ability to judge justly. Because of this, the smaller our view of Him, the more likely we'll be to harbor bitterness and unforgiveness in our hearts. So what do we do about this difficulty? If we're honest and recognize that our view of God is too small for us to release this person into His hands, where can we develop a bigger view of Him? Our view of God grows as we study Scripture. It's in the Bible that we see God on display—in all His power, glory, and strength.

As He reveals Himself to us through Scripture, our trust in Him will grow. One of the direct consequences of this will be our increased ability to entrust to Him the people who have hurt us. We'll be able to let go. We'll be able to forgive.

Choosing to forgive is a matter of the will. It is saying that you will no longer bring up the offense, play around with it in your mind, or throw it in the person's face. It is letting go, refusing to rehearse or rehash the hurt. It is no longer wanting to hurt the person because he or she hurt you. Forgiveness is not a onetime thing. As we learn new things about how the hurt is affecting us, we have to re-forgive. We can't forgive what we don't know. As the consequences develop, we have to forgive each time—not because the original forgiveness was insincere, but because it's a process.

What does forgiveness not *mean? It's important to remember that forgiving someone doesn't mean that you throw common sense out the door and continue in a relationship that is unhealthy. Forgiveness does not mean enabling. If the hurt has been caused by destructive behavior, it is essential that you set boundaries for the future that will protect you. Get to the root of anything that was unhealthy in the relationship and fix it. Make new rules; set new parameters. You can forgive and demand that it never happen again.*

Forgiveness does not let the other person off the hook with God. God is a God of justice, and He will deal with the person who has hurt you, in this life or in the next. Choosing to forgive means that I am no longer the enforcer; God is. If a punishment needs to be doled out, He will do it. Each time I'm triggered and can feel the anger returning, I need to say, "Whoa—this no longer belongs to me. It belongs to God." Give it to Him again.

Is there someone in your life whom you need to forgive? Can you hand that person over to God, asking Him to judge justly? Can you release your grip on the need to see justice served today, before your eyes? Can you trust God's timing? Come to God in prayer, and ask Him to help you. Ask Him to cleanse you of your bitterness. Ask Him to heal the hurt. He came to bind up the brokenhearted. How He loves you and longs to bring you to a place of freedom. Unforgiveness keeps you chained to the past, a victim of its pain. Forgiveness frees you to move beyond it and experience peace of soul.

Day Four
THE DAVIDIC COVENANT AND THE MESSIAH

Read 2 Samuel 7:1–17.

1. Where was the Ark of God? What did David want to do? Did God grant him his heart's desire? Why or why not? See 2 Samuel 7:1–13.

2. It's easy to imagine the disappointment David felt when he was told that his dream of building God a temple wouldn't happen. What words of comfort did God speak to David at this time? See 2 Samuel 7:12–16.

The promise made to David in 2 Samuel 7:16 is known as the Davidic Covenant. This covenant was a binding agreement that God made with David. It depended on God's faithfulness, not David's descendants' performance.

3. When God said that David's kingdom would never end, it became public knowledge. His promise wasn't kept on the quiet. It became a lifeline of hope for the Israelite people during the times when their circumstances made it look like all was lost. Psalm 89 was written hundreds of years after God made this covenant with David. Jerusalem had been destroyed. No Davidic king was reigning there. In this psalm, the Israelite people were appealing to God to remain faithful to His promises in the wake of their defeat. They held up His promises, one by one. What were the promises they were clinging to? Read Psalm 89:4–5 and 20–38 (NAB).

4. The Davidic Covenant promised that there would be a kingdom that would last forever, and that one of David's descendants would sit on its throne. Jewish theologians believed that this ruler, called the Messiah,[8] would bring spiritual and national restoration to Israel. The precise understanding of the Messiah's attributes would evolve and develop over time. When the political situation intensified for the Israelites under the oppression of the Romans in 63 BC, the desire to search out the prophecies of the Old Testament for insight into the Messiah intensified. The Jewish people were clinging to the promise of a Messiah king who would restore their nation. Read the following verses, and note what insight they provided regarding the awaited Messiah and His connection to David.

Taken from Saint Peter's speech at Pentecost:

> For [in Psalm 16:8–11] David says concerning [the Messiah], "I saw the Lord always before me, for he is at my right hand that I may not be shaken; therefore my heart was glad, and my tongue rejoiced; moreover my flesh will dwell in hope. For you will not abandon my soul to Hades, nor let your Holy One see corruption. You have made known to me the ways of life; you will make me full of gladness with your presence." Brethren, I may say to you confidently of the patriarch David that he both died and was buried, and his tomb is with us to this day. Being therefore a prophet, and knowing that God had sworn with an oath to him that he would set one of his descendants upon his throne, he foresaw and spoke of the resurrection of the Christ, that he was not abandoned to Hades, nor did his flesh see corruption. (Acts 2:25–31)

> "For to us a child is born, to us a son is given; and the government will be upon his shoulder, and his name will be called 'Wonderful Counselor, Mighty God, Everlasting Father, Prince of Peace.' Of the increase of his government and of peace there will be no end, upon the throne of David, and over his kingdom, to establish it, and to uphold it with justice and righteousness from this time forth and for evermore" (Isaiah 9:6–7).

---

[8] The words *Messiah* and *Christ* mean "anointed."

David | 2

Read these two passages together to gain the full insight needed:

"The Lord said to Samuel, 'How long will you grieve over Saul, seeing I have rejected him from being king over Israel? Fill your horn with oil, and go; I will send you to Jesse the Bethlehemite, for I have provided for myself a king among his sons'" (1 Samuel 16:1). "And [Jesse] sent, and brought him in. Now he was ruddy, and had beautiful eyes, and was handsome. And the Lord said, 'Arise, anoint him; for this is he.'" (1 Samuel 16:12)

"But you, O Bethlehem Eph´rathah, who are little to be among the clans of Judah, from you shall come forth for me one who is to be ruler in Israel, whose origin is from of old, from ancient days. Therefore he shall give them up until the time when she who has labor pains has brought forth; then the rest of his brethren shall return to the sons of Israel. And he shall stand and feed his flock in the strength of the LORD, in the majesty of the name of the LORD his God. And they shall dwell secure, for now he shall be great to the ends of the earth. And this shall be peace" (Micah 5:2-4).

5. A. What proof do we have that the Jews were still clinging to the promise made to David at the time of Christ's birth? See Matthew 2:1–6.

   B. What was the consequence of the chief priests and scribes sharing this information with Herod? See Matthew 2:7–18.

Quiet your heart and enjoy His presence. . . . Wait at His feet.

Between the first promise of the Messiah in Genesis (3:14–15) and Jesus' arrival recorded in the Gospel of Matthew, there are many stories of hardship and setbacks. Throughout their journey, the Jewish people clung to the hope that God would one day bring a deliverer. Waiting can be the hardest thing in the world to do. Sometimes events make it appear that all is lost. Imagine what the Jewish people felt when the soldiers swept through Bethlehem, killing all the baby boys. Their circumstances certainly tempted them to assume that God had forgotten them. Yet a remnant always chose hope in God over despair.

We all will experience seasons in life when we have to wait. The question is, will we still trust in God's promises when we don't see evidence of His hand at work? Will we resist the urge to take matters into our own hands? Will we continue to pray, even when it seems our prayers aren't being answered? Will we acknowledge that God's ways are not our ways, that His timing is perfect, and His plan is always the best one?

Never forget that the darkest hour of the night is the one before dawn. At the very point that the Jewish people might have thought all was lost, their Savior had come. As you wait, cling to God's promises. Follow the psalmist's example and hold those promises up to Him in prayer. Call on Him in faith to fulfill them in your life. If God hasn't given you a clear sense of something you should do to help the situation, resist the urge to take matters into your own hands. "The Lord will fight for you, and you have only to be still" (Exodus 14:14). Wait patiently. Wait prayerfully. Your Wonder-Counselor, God-Hero, Father-Forever, Prince of Peace will not disappoint.

Day Five
THE PROMISE KEEPER

Read Luke 2:1–5.

1. Both Mary and Joseph were descendants of King David, as seen in the genealogies of Saint Matthew and Saint Luke. (Joseph's genealogy is found in Matthew 1:1–16, and tradition holds that the genealogy in Luke 3 is that of Mary.) God had chosen Mary to carry the Messiah and bring Him into the world. But there was a problem. Mary was from Nazareth. What event occurred to fulfill God's promise that the Messiah would not only be a descendant of King David but would also be born in Bethlehem, the town of David?

Could it be that God was at work in the heart of Caesar Augustus, prompting him to make a decision that would relocate thousands of people, just so He could fulfill the promise He had made to David centuries before? What lesson do we learn from this? We learn that God keeps His promises. Friends may let you down. Husbands may be unfaithful. Children may fail to follow through on what they've said they'd do. But God is different. He will move heaven and earth to remain faithful to His promises to you.

2. What do the following verses reveal about God's character? See Numbers 23:19, Titus 1:2, Hebrews 6:18, and CCC 215.

3. The fact that God keeps His promises has enormous implications for our lives. It should change the way we live. Why? Because God's promises provide us with a foundation that cannot be shaken. Regardless of what is going on in our lives, there is a promise from God that we can claim and stand on. Meditate on the following promises of God. Which one is the most meaningful to you in your present circumstances?

"He gives power to the faint, and to him who has no might he increases strength. Even youths shall faint and be weary, and young men shall fall exhausted; but they who wait for the Lord shall renew their strength, they shall mount up with wings like eagles, they shall run and not be weary, they shall walk and not faint" (Isaiah 40:29–31).

"For I know the plans I have for you, says the Lord, plans for welfare and not for evil, to give you a future and a hope" (Jeremiah 29:11).

"Come to me, all who labor and are heavy laden, and I will give you rest. Take my yoke upon you, and learn from me; for I am gentle and lowly in heart, and you will find rest for your souls" (Matthew 11:28–29).

"For the wages of sin is death, but the free gift of God is eternal life in Christ Jesus our Lord" (Romans 6:23).

"We know that in everything God works for good with those who love him, who are called according to his purpose" (Romans 8:28).

"No, in all these things we are more than conquerors through him who loved us. For I am sure that neither death, nor life, nor angels, nor principalities, nor things present, nor things to come, nor powers, nor height, nor depth, nor anything else in all creation, will be able to separate us from the love of God in Christ Jesus our Lord" (Romans 8:37–39).

"No temptation has overtaken you that is not common to man. God is faithful, and he will not let you be tempted beyond your strength, but with the temptation will also provide the way of escape, that you may be able to endure it" (1 Corinthians 10:13).

"And my God will supply every need of yours according to his riches in glory in Christ Jesus" (Philippians 4:19).

"If we confess our sins, he is faithful and just, and will forgive our sins and cleanse us from all unrighteousness" (1 John 1:9).

4. Where do all the promises of God in the Old and New Testaments find their fulfillment? See 2 Corinthians 1:19–20.

Quiet your heart and enjoy His presence. . . . He will never let you down.

If we really believe that God is faithful to His promises, it should change the way we live. It should stop the up-and-down, yo-yo cycle of sometimes feeling spiritually strong and sometimes feeling low.

Do you want to have a stable, steady walk with Christ? Then increase your study of Scripture. Make saturating yourself with the Bible one of the highest priorities in your life. Place it above exercise. Place it above your to-do list. Make this the first place you turn every morning.

Why give Scripture such a high place of importance? When we don't know Scripture, our spiritual lives can become very connected to our emotions. Our spiritual stability will go up and down, dependent on how we feel. Periods of crisis or disappointment or spiritual dryness will hit, and then we'll pray, and we'll tend to measure the effectiveness of our prayers. Since God rarely responds within minutes to our requests, we'll begin to analyze our emotions. "Do I feel that God comforted me?" we'll ask ourselves. "Do I feel strong?" When we don't feel better, we often start to doubt God. "He's not helping me! Where is He? I don't feel Him!" Discouragement or panic can result. We'll be tempted to take matters into our own hands. Our desire for control will escalate, and our peace will vanish.

How different it can be when we are rooted in Scripture. When we have saturated our heads and hearts with the Bible, when we know God's promises and cling to them, we react differently to crisis, disappointment, and spiritual dryness. When we need God's intervention in our lives, we go to prayer and to Scripture, and then ask ourselves, "Do I know that God is at work, keeping His promises, regardless of how I feel?"

Take some time to talk to God about one specific promise He has made in Scripture. Present your needs to Him in light of that promise and His character.

Conclusion

We long to be women after God's own heart. What greater words of praise could there be? What a relief it is that God is faithfully working within us, and that His promises are strong, even when our hearts are weak.

With all the best intentions to be holy and good, we are going to fall. And when we do, it's going to hurt. There will always be a temptation to respond by self-justifying, blaming, or giving up.

Both David and Jesus dare us to live differently. Their examples challenge us to be brave and keep going. David fell morally, but his response to his failure drew him closer to God, not further away. His confession was honest and heartfelt. Jesus fell under the weight of the cross. It wasn't His fault—He had done nothing wrong—but He couldn't make it to Calvary without stumbling. Jesus' response was to feel His way back up, one hand over the other, and to persevere.

When we fall, we have a choice. We can crumple and try to hide behind a mask of fake perfection, pretending that we have it more together than we really do. Or we can *own* our weakness, *own* our story, and believe with all our hearts that out of ashes, God can and will create something beautiful. We can trust in the yes of His promises, which guarantees that no matter how bad something looks, there is always hope because of God. Courage can rise in the face of failure. In fact, resurrection can only occur if something has died, if something has fallen onto the ground in the first place.

Invite God to breathe life into the places where you feel fallen, weak, and ashamed. Lift your eyes to His face, and see your Abba Father smiling upon you. He embraces your story as the journey that it is. Ask Him for a fresh experience of His unconditional love. Just as David danced before the Ark of the Covenant, let your soul dance in the presence of the One who adores you.

My Resolution

In what specific way will I apply what I learned in this lesson?

Examples:

1. I'll take some time to reflect on my friendships. Have I chosen to go deep with people who challenge me to be more like Christ? Am I being positively influenced by the women I am closest to? Is there someone in my life whom I can trust to

speak to me truthfully? Because it's difficult to speak the truth in love, I will proactively give him or her permission to hold me accountable in the areas of my spiritual life where I most want to progress.

2. When I feel tempted to wallow in the pit of self-pity, I will instead go to confession and receive God's mercy.

3. I will write down the promise of God that is most meaningful to me today. I'll carry it with me, in my pocket or my purse, to remind me continually of God's faithfulness. I have a choice regarding what I dwell on. I'll choose to dwell on God's truth instead of my emotions.

My resolution:

Catechism Clips

CCC 85 "The task of giving an authentic interpretation of the Word of God, whether in its written form or in the form of Tradition, has been entrusted to the living teaching office of the Church alone. Its authority in this matter is exercised in the name of Jesus Christ." This means that the task of interpretation has been entrusted to the bishops in communion with the successor of Peter, the Bishop of Rome.

CCC 86 "Yet this Magisterium is not superior to the Word of God, but is its servant. It teaches only what has been handed on to it. At the divine command and with the help of the Holy Spirit, it listens to this devoutly, guards it with dedication and expounds it faithfully. All that it proposes for belief as being divinely revealed is drawn from this single deposit of faith."

CCC 215 "The sum of your word is truth; and every one of your righteous ordinances endures forever." "And now, O Lord God, you are God, and your words are true"; this is why God's promises always come true. God is Truth itself, whose words cannot deceive. This is why one can abandon oneself in full trust to the truth and faithfulness of his word in all things. The beginning of sin and of man's fall was due to a lie of the tempter who induced doubt of God's word, kindness and faithfulness.

CCC 2579 David is par excellence the king "after God's own heart," the shepherd who prays for his people and prays in their name. His submission to the will of God, his praise, and his repentance, will be a model for the prayer of the people. His prayer, the prayer of God's Anointed, is a faithful adherence to the divine promise and expresses a loving and joyful trust in God, the only King and Lord. In the Psalms David, inspired by the Holy Spirit, is the first prophet of Jewish and Christian prayer. The prayer of Christ, the true Messiah and Son of David, will reveal and fulfill the meaning of this prayer.

Verse Study

See Appendix 3 for instructions on how to complete a verse study.

1 Chronicles 28:9

1. Verse:

2. Paraphrase:

3. Questions:

4. Cross-references:

5. Personal Application:

NOTES

Lesson 3

PSALM 23

Introduction

Four-year-old Laeka looked at Amy with wide eyes of shock. They had just left Vacation Bible School, and Amy was explaining what she had learned that day. "Jesus is the Good Shepherd, and we're the sheep!" she announced. "We're *sheep*?" said Laeka in horror. "I thought we were human beings!" The whole idea of a metaphor was completely lost on him.

We may not like being considered sheep any more than Laeka did. A short study of sheep reveals that it's not a very complimentary comparison. Sheep are among the most stupid of animals. They are utterly defenseless. If an attacker comes toward them, all they can do is run away. They fall down and can't get back up. They'll wander in circles, grazing on brown, inferior pasture until they are led to a better place. Left to their own devices, they are helpless and hopeless.

When we put aside our pride and accept that we're sheep, we stop relying on ourselves and allow ourselves to be led by the Good Shepherd. We acknowledge our weakness and our need for God. And the Good Shepherd treasures us! He loves us so much that He gave His life to keep us safe.

When David wrote the 23rd Psalm, he wrote from experience. In the years before he was anointed the King of Israel, he had been a shepherd. He knew firsthand both how needy sheep are and what is required of a good shepherd. When predators tried to attack his flock, he showed his love for them by doing whatever was necessary to protect them. When David was convincing King Saul that he had the courage to stand up to Goliath, he said, "Your servant used to keep sheep for his father; and when there came a lion, or a bear, and took a lamb from the flock, I went after him and struck him and delivered it out of his mouth; and if it arose against me, I caught him by his beard, and struck him and killed him" (1 Samuel 17:34–35).

Psalm 23, the most familiar of all the psalms, has comforted countless people throughout the centuries. When we repeat the beautiful words, "The Lord is my shepherd," we are declaring our dependence on God. We're safe because God promises that He will "will supply every need of yours according to his riches in glory in Christ Jesus" (Philippians 4:19). God always keeps His promises, and that is the truest source of comfort.

Day One
"THE LORD IS MY SHEPHERD, I SHALL NOT WANT."

Read Psalm 23.

1. Psalm 23:1 doesn't say, "The Lord is *a* shepherd," or "The Lord is *our* shepherd." It says, "The Lord is *my* shepherd." What is the significance of this word choice?

2. In John 10:11, Jesus said, "I am the good shepherd." What insight is gained from the following verses regarding our Good Shepherd?

    Luke 15:4–7

    John 10:11–15

3. In order to protect his flock, a shepherd would create a sheep pen out of rocks or branches, with a single entrance. At night, he'd lead the sheep into the enclosure and would sleep across the entrance in order to defend them. Knowing this, how do you interpret John 10:7: "So Jesus said to them, 'Truly, truly, I say to you, I am the door of the sheep'"?

4. As much as we want to be totally free- completely self-sufficient- the captains of our own souls— the reality is, everyone serves someone. We end up serving what we love the most. This means that we have a choice in whom we serve. We either serve Jesus, the Good Shepherd, and accept that He's the One in charge, or we serve people or things that definitely do *not* have our best interests at heart. What are the qualities of our Good Shepherd that make it easier to give Him control of our lives?

5. It's interesting that David wrote, "The Lord is my shepherd, I shall not want," when he had experienced so many years of scarcity and difficulty. He had been hunted by King Saul and forced to live as a fugitive, and later was pursued by his own estranged son, Absalom. He had experienced seasons of need. So what did David mean when he wrote, "I shall not want"? Was he suggesting that if you trust in the Lord, you'll never be hungry and will always have what you want? See Philippians 4:19.

Quiet your heart and enjoy His presence. . . . There is nothing you lack if you have Him.

Ahhh . . . contentment. That seemingly elusive quality so connected to inner peace. Without it, we are on a fast track to misery. With it, we have abiding joy that can't be taken from us. What do you feel is blocking your personal contentment? Can you name it? So often, we assume contentment comes from the lifting of difficulty, or the receipt of something longed for. But that's not how it works. True contentment comes when we quit acting like discontented sheep, standing at the gate and noticing how green the grass is on the other side. It comes when we look up at our Shepherd and trust that He can see farther than we can, and He is giving us everything we need in this moment. It comes when we accept our life as is, as what His hands have provided. We may not like our circumstances. Our life may be filled with grief, hurt, and pain. When this is the case, our Good Shepherd asks us to come to Him, so He can offer comfort and hope.

Make no mistake, God is deeply concerned about you and what you are longing for. He can see when your motive is pure—when your desire is a good one. But He asks that you trust Him and His timing. The bigger your view of God, the easier this will be. The more you grow in awareness of His majesty, the complexity and faithfulness of His plans, and His limitless love, the more you'll accept and believe that He is a God worthy of your trust.

Take some time to talk to God about what stands in the way of your contentment. Explain to the One who knows and loves you like no other why this matters so much to you. Then place it at His feet. Tell Him that you trust Him with this, your greatest desire. Ask Him to fill your heart with contentment. Ask Him to help you grow so that more and more, you desire what He wants. Every time your heart aches in longing, go back to Him, and give it to Him again. The desire will be safe with Him. He will not forget. He is your Good Shepherd, and He promises to provide all that you need.

Day Two
"HE MAKES ME LIE DOWN IN GREEN PASTURES. HE LEADS ME BESIDE STILL WATERS."

Read Psalm 23:2.

1. Psalm 23:2 says that the shepherd "makes me" lie down in green pastures. Wouldn't you think that lying down in green pastures would be the natural inclination of a sheep? The truth is, sheep will refuse to lie down if they are afraid, hungry, experiencing friction within the herd, or being bothered by pests. No matter how lush and beautiful their surroundings, they'll rest only when they are free from these things. The only thing that brings them comfort is the presence of

the shepherd. In what ways are you like the sheep who find it hard to lie down in green pastures? What steals your inner peace? What keeps you up at night, robbing you of much-needed rest?

2. When the shepherd stands in the midst of the herd of sheep, the sheep instantly are calmer. They know they are defenseless, so having their protector physically close soothes them. How might the following verses offer you comfort when you are afraid? See Psalm 34:8, CCC 336, and Psalm 121.

3. A good shepherd leads his sheep to the best places to graze. Left on their own, sheep will never find good pasture, and will continuously be on their feet, looking for something to satisfy their hunger. Sometimes the shepherd has to remove rocks and roots and stumps in order to create the lush land his sheep need. What sort of inferior land might you settle for when your soul is hungry? What are the rocks, roots, and stumps that God needs to remove in your heart so that you can freely feed on what He is providing?

The following words of Christian author Peter Kreeft are certainly thought provoking: "We *want* to complexify our lives. We don't have to, we *want* to. We wanted to be harried and hassled and busy. Unconsciously, we want the very things we complain about. For if we had leisure, we would look at ourselves and listen to our

4. The friction that sheep experience within a herd certainly lacks the sophistication of human tension, jealousy, and rivalry. Yet the solution is the same. Our eyes can only be in one place at a time. Either they are on Christ the Good Shepherd, or they are on someone or something else. What insight do we gain into this issue from John 10:27?

5. When sheep are agitated by pests, a good shepherd will treat his sheep with insect repellent or dip them in medication to take care of whatever is eating at them. Our Good Shepherd is no different. When He sees circumstances aggravating us, He comes and ministers to us, treating our "bites" and covering us with protection. Which part of the Trinity ministers to us in this way? See CCC 1695.

Quiet your heart and enjoy His presence. . . . Let Him restore your soul.

After making his sheep lie down in green pastures, the shepherd leads them to still waters. He knows where their thirst will truly be satisfied. Sheep can actually survive for months without drinking from a pool of water if there is dew on the grass where they are feeding. But to drink this dew, they have to get up early.[10] There is a replenishing dew available to us each morning. Jesus calls out to us, "If any one thirst, let him come to me and drink" (John 7:37). He promises to restore our souls each and every day. Do you long for this refreshing gift of His presence? Turn the words of this hymn into a prayer: "Dear Lord and Father of mankind, Drop thy still dews of quietness, till all our strivings cease; take from our souls the strain and stress, and let our ordered lives confess the beauty of thy peace."

---

[9] Peter Kreeft, *Christianity for Modern Pagans* (San Francisco: Ignatius Press, 1993), 168.
[10] W. Phillip Keller, *A Shepherd Looks at Psalm 23* (Grand Rapids, MI: Zondervan, 2007), 60.

Day Three
"HE LEADS ME IN PATHS OF RIGHEOUSNESS FOR HIS NAME'S SAKE."

Read Psalm 23:3.

If sheep are not *led* down paths to fresh pasture, they will stay put. They'll remain in their favorite grazing spots and eat until there is nothing left—even eating the roots of the grass, so that the land ends up ruined. The result? Malnourished sheep and eroded soil. Because of this, it's very important for a shepherd to keep his flock on the move, making sure that they are following a plan of rotation on fresh pasture. The shepherd has the big picture. He sees all of his land and the advantages and disadvantages of each area. He wisely leads his sheep down a certain path to the right place at the right time. He does this out of love for the sheep, but also for the sake of his name. His reputation as a good shepherd is on the line.

1. We get tempted, just like the sheep, to stay where it's comfortable. Has God called you to move on to a new, higher pasture? Is He asking you to take a spiritual step of growth and maturity? What is it? How does Hebrews 5:11–6:1 warn us about growing complacent in our walk with Christ?

2. In Mark 8:34, our Good Shepherd described the path we will need to walk if we decide we want to follow Him to spiritual maturity. Put this verse into your own words.

3. To deny yourself and take up your cross is a truly countercultural, radical way to live. You may be called to swim against the tide. In our strongly individualistic society, selfishness runs rampant. We pay lip service to loving one another, but more often than not, we can remain stuck in unhealthy love of self—self-

absorption and preoccupation with self (i.e., the me, *me*, ME syndrome). How does Christ ask us to live in John 13:34?

4. When God calls His people to higher pasture, few follow. It's rarely because we don't understand what He is asking. We just don't feel like doing it. Our excuses might sound a lot fancier than that, but the bottom line is, we want to be the ones in charge. We don't want to follow. We want to be the shepherd, not the sheep. Read the following quotes from the saints on obedience. Record any inspiration you gain from their words.

"I often thought my constitution would never endure the work I had to do, [but] the Lord said to me: 'Daughter, obedience gives strength.'"[11]
—Saint Teresa of Ávila, Doctor of the Church

"The Devil doesn't fear austerity but holy obedience."[12] —Saint Francis de Sales

"All that is done by obedience is meritorious. . . . It is obedience, which, by the light of Faith, puts self-will to death, and causes the obedient man to despise his own will and throw himself into the arms of his superior. . . . Placed in the bark of obedience, he passes happily through the stormy sea of this life, in peace of soul and tranquility of heart. Obedience and faith disperse darkness; he is strong because he has no longer any weakness or fears, for self-will, which is the cause of inordinate fear and weakness, has been destroyed."[13]
—Saint Catherine of Siena, Doctor of the Church

"A single instant passed under simple obedience is immeasurably more valuable in the sight of God than an entire day spent in the most sublime contemplation."[14]
—Saint Mary Magdalene de Pazzi

---

[11] http://www.whitelilyoftrinity.com/saints_quotes_obedience.html.
[12] Ibid.
[13] Ibid.
[14] Ibid.

5. The path to follow Christ can seem overwhelming. One might even say it's impossible. And it would be, if it weren't for the gift of the indwelling Holy Spirit. The divine power of the Holy Spirit gives us everything we need to live a life of devotion to God (2 Peter 1:3–4). So what would you say to someone who says that she doesn't feel like the Holy Spirit is making a difference in her life? See CCC 1265 and 1266 and Acts 5:32.

Quiet your heart and enjoy His presence. . . . Let Him guide you on the right paths.

When God leads us down paths that are difficult, we have a choice in terms of how we react. Many people shake their fists at God, demanding an explanation for the divergence from what they desire. This is the easy response. It's the natural one. Our human nature makes us long to understand. We want to see the meaning behind what we experience. It takes a great deal of self-denial to trust God when we don't like the path He chooses for us. But when we remain confident in Him and in His love despite our circumstances, we have made the supreme act of love. It consoles the heart of Christ. The greatest gift we can give to Him is an obedient, trustful surrender to His will in our lives. Author Nancy Guthrie calls this act of surrender "giving ourselves over to the goodness of God." The more we know Jesus as the Good Shepherd, the easier it'll be to offer Him this gift. Remember that He has the big picture. He's aware of the advantages and disadvantages of each circumstance and how it'll affect our growth in holiness. He wisely leads each of us down a certain path to the right place at the right time, always for our benefit, and for the sake of His name.

Day Four
"EVEN THOUGH I WALK THROUGH THE VALLEY OF THE SHADOW OF DEATH, I FEAR NO EVIL; FOR YOU ARE WITH ME; YOUR ROD AND YOUR STAFF, THEY COMFORT ME."

Read Psalm 23:4.

Each summer, shepherds in Israel would drive their sheep up into the hill country. As they slowly wound higher and higher, they would pass through valleys. These valleys were dangerous places where predators waited to attack. There were risks of mudslides, avalanches, chilling storms, and floods. This was a time of intense intimacy with the shepherd, because he was the only one accompanying the sheep on the journey.

1. There is a grammatical change between Psalm 23:1 and 23:4. What is it, and why is it significant?

2. While we wish we could hop from one mountaintop experience to the next, there will always be valleys. Sometimes our valley experiences are similar to those of the sheep, in that the pain or grief is so intense that no person can accompany us there. But even in the most distressing circumstance, we are assured in Psalm 23:4 that we don't need to be afraid. God never said that we wouldn't face danger. But He promised that He would always be with us. This was His message to His people from the beginning of Scripture to the end. Read the following verses, recording your thoughts regarding the difference it makes to face what we fear with our Shepherd by our side.

   Deuteronomy 31:6

   Isaiah 41:10

   Matthew 28:20

   Hebrews 13:5–6

3. "I am with you." That is what God has always said to anyone who is afraid. He promises that no matter what we face, whether the mess we are in is our fault or not, He will never leave us. He will protect us. Statements like that don't mean very much unless you have a lot of power to back them up. Fortunately for us,

God does. Read verse 4 of the psalm. The shepherd's rod was a club, often with nails in one end of it. It was a weapon. It wasn't used on the sheep; it was used against predators to protect the sheep. Shepherds could throw the rod with incredible accuracy. What is it about God that can protect us the way a shepherd can protect his sheep with his rod? See Daniel 4:32.

4. Sheep don't only succumb to dangers from outside the fold. Sometimes they just wander off and end up on the edge of a cliff. They can drink from water that's fetid and full of disease. And so another very important part of the shepherd's job is to protect the sheep from themselves. This is where the staff is used. The shepherd's staff is a long pole with a crook at the top, and it's used to pull the sheep back to a place of safety, back to the shepherd's side. What are some examples of "staffs" that God uses to protect us?

Matthew 18:10 and Psalm 91:12

CCC 890 and 896

Quiet your heart and enjoy His presence. . . . He is with us in the valleys.

Time spent in the valley can be some of the most precious moments or seasons we'll experience with the Lord. Why is this? So often the Shepherd's presence is felt more keenly in the valley. This is where we learn about our Savior's all-sufficiency. This is the time when all the things we've learned are put to the test, and we find that if we will trust Him, God is always enough. We don't need to fear whatever comes, because God goes before us. He sees the big picture, and always leads us to the best places. When the places that He has deemed best feel like a big mistake, He stands right beside us, assuring us of His love. Sheep are very timid. The only reason they have confidence to walk through the valley is the shepherd's presence. God offers us that same security.

Day Five
"YOU PREPARE A TABLE BEFORE ME IN THE PRESENCE OF MY ENEMIES; YOU ANOINT MY HEAD WITH OIL, MY CUP OVERFLOWS."

Read Psalm 23:5.

Shepherds "prepare a table" for their sheep on the mesas (the high plateaus). These were wonderful grazing lands, but they needed to be prepped by the shepherd before the sheep could go there. The shepherd would go ahead, looking for poisonous plants that needed pulling and keeping a watchful eye for any predators. Even with the shepherd's sharp eye, there was always the possibility that a predator would remain hidden up on the rimrock, waiting for a sheep to roam a little too far from the shepherd. Because an attack would come swiftly, the safest place to be was as close to the shepherd as possible.

1. Our Good Shepherd knows every trick of our enemy, recognizing that "[our] adversary the devil prowls around like a roaring lion, seeking some one to devour" (1 Peter 5:8). Jesus has gone before us, experiencing the attacks and temptations of the devil. He knows what is needed in order for us to remain strong and faithful. Our Good Shepherd sets a table for us in front of our enemies (Psalm 23:5) and places on the table all that we need to be nourished, strengthened, and protected. It's up to us to eat what He offers. The following verses reveal two of the things that are on the table. What are they?

    John 6:54

    Jeremiah 15:16

2. When you walk forward to the Eucharistic feast, do you appreciate what it cost Christ to prepare this sacred meal for you? List below some of the sacrifices He made.

3. Shepherds would anoint the heads of the sheep with oil in order to repel insects and soothe wounds. The oil provided both protection and comfort. Anointing with oil has rich meaning in the sacraments. What does it signify in baptism, the anointing of the sick, confirmation, and ordination? See CCC 1294.

4. When a person is anointed with oil in confirmation, he or she is receiving a mark, or seal. Whose seal marks the confirmand? What does being marked with a seal mean? See CCC 1295 and 1296. What does this mean to you?

5. Our Good Shepherd prepares us a table filled with provisions, keeps an eye out for predators, and pours the oil of His Holy Spirit over us, marking us as His own. As long as we keep our perspective on all that He has given us, we'll always agree with the psalmist that our "cup overflows" with blessings from Christ. Make a list of your blessings, both spiritual (Ephesians 1:3–10) and material.

Quiet your heart and enjoy His presence. . . . He pours blessings on us without ceasing.

Ann Voskamp gives beautiful insight into the fruit that comes from a thankful heart in her book One Thousand Gifts:

In the original language, "he gave thanks" reads "eucharisteo." I underline it on the page. . . . The root word of eucharisteo is charis, *meaning "grace." Jesus took the bread and saw it as grace and gave thanks. He took the bread and knew it to be a gift and gave thanks. But there is more, and I read it. Eucharisteo, thanksgiving, envelopes the Greek word for grace,* charis. *But it also holds its derivative, the Greek word* chara, *meaning "joy." Joy. Ah . . . yes. I might be needing me some of that. That might be what the quest for more is all about— that which Augustine claimed, "Without exception . . . all try their hardest to reach the same goal, that is, joy . . ."*

Joy. But where can I seize this holy grail of joy? I look back down to the page. Was this the clue to the quest of all most important? Deep chara *joy is found only at the table of the* euCHARisteo—*the table of thanksgiving. I sat there long . . . wondering . . . is it that simple?*

Is the height of my chara *joy dependent on the depths of my eucharisteo thanks?*

So then as long as thanks is possible . . . I think this through. **As long as thanks is possible, then joy is always possible. Joy is always possible.** *Wherever, meaning—now; wherever, meaning—here. The holy grail of joy is not in some exotic location or some emotional mountain peak experience. The joy wonder could be here! Here, in the messy, piercing ache of now, joy might be—unbelievably—possible!* [15]

Take some time to talk to the Lord about your desire for joy. Ask His forgiveness for any ingratitude or discontent in your heart. Meditate on your blessings and ask the Lord to fill you with a spirit of thanksgiving.

Conclusion

"Surely goodness and mercy shall follow me all the days of my life; and I shall dwell in the house of the LORD *for ever" (Psalm 23:6).*

A sheep who is in the care of an attentive shepherd is in a privileged position. He can rest, because goodness and mercy, embodied in the shepherd, are continuously present.

How many of us confidently say, "Goodness and mercy shall follow me all the days of my life"? It's not hard to have this attitude when everything is going well. But what about when our loved one suffers wasting disease, or there isn't enough money to pay the bills, or a child rebels, or a husband is unfaithful, or the demands on us mount and the pressure builds? At those times, we're tempted to say, "Panic and worry will pursue me all the days of my life."

Yet the truth is, no matter our circumstances, the love of Christ always pursues us. He *is* goodness and mercy. When we foolishly think that we could survive better on our own, He chases us and calls us home. Jesus said, "What man of you, having a hundred sheep, if he has lost one of them, does not leave the ninety-nine in the

---

[15] Ann Voskamp, *One Thousand Gifts* (Grand Rapids, MI: Zondervan, 2010), 32–3.

wilderness, and go after the one which is lost, until he finds it? And when he has found it, he lays it on his shoulders, rejoicing. And when he comes home, he calls together his friends and his neighbors, saying to them, 'Rejoice with me, for I have found my sheep which was lost'" (Luke 15:4–6).

He longs for us to trust that He is in our tomorrows. We don't need to fear the future, because He goes before us. Either He will remove the obstacles and shield us from suffering or He will be everlasting arms beneath us, giving us the strength to walk through. And one day, we will dwell in His heavenly home, a place free from sorrow and pain. This is where all our longings will be fulfilled. *Don't expect earth to feel like heaven. God has never promised that. What He promises is His presence.* Our Good Shepherd assures us that He will stand in our midst, He'll come after us if we wander, and He'll go ahead of us to prepare a place of eternal joy and rest. And this is the most abundant life imaginable.

> Christ with me, Christ before me, Christ behind me,
> Christ in me, Christ beneath me, Christ above me,
> Christ on my right, Christ on my left,
> Christ when I lie down, Christ when I sit down,
> Christ in the heart of every man who thinks of me,
> Christ in the mouth of every man who speaks of me,
> Christ in the eye that sees me,
> Christ in the ear that hears me.[16] —Saint Patrick

My Resolution

In what specific way will I apply what I learned in this lesson?

Examples:

1. I'll begin a journal of my blessings to help me recognize the ways in which God's goodness and mercy pursue me every day.

2. When I go forward to the table my Good Shepherd has prepared for me, I will think about what it cost Him to offer me His body and blood in the Eucharist.

---

[16] "St. Patrick," GoodReads, http://www.goodreads.com/quotes/413139-christ-with-me-christ-before-me-christ-behind-me-christ.

3. I believe God is asking me to go to higher ground with Him. He wants me to take a spiritual step of growth and maturity. I will remember the words of Saint Teresa of Ávila: "Obedience gives strength." This week, I'll take a concrete step to obey God in this area of my life.

My resolution:

Catechism Clips

CCC 336 From its beginning until death, human life is surrounded by their watchful care and intercession. "Beside each believer stands an angel as protector and shepherd leading him to life." Already here on earth the Christian life shares by faith in the blessed company of angels and men united in God.

CCC 890 The mission of the Magisterium is linked to the definitive nature of the covenant established by God with his people in Christ. It is this Magisterium's task to preserve God's people from deviations and defections and to guarantee them the objective possibility of professing the true faith without error. Thus, the pastoral duty of the Magisterium is aimed at seeing to it that the People of God abides in the truth that liberates. To fulfill this service, Christ endowed the Church's shepherds with the charism of infallibility in matters of faith and morals.

CCC 896 The Good Shepherd ought to be the model and "form" of the bishop's pastoral office. Conscious of his own weaknesses, "the bishop . . . can have compassion for those who are ignorant and erring. He should not refuse to listen to his subjects whose welfare he promotes as of his very own children. . . . The faithful . . . should be closely attached to the bishop as the Church is to Jesus Christ, and as Jesus Christ is to the Father":

> Let all follow the bishop, as Jesus Christ follows his Father, and the college of presbyters as the apostles; respect the deacons as you do God's law. Let no one do anything concerning the Church in separation from the bishop.

CCC 1265 Baptism not only purifies from all sins, but also makes the neophyte "a new creature," an adopted son of God, who has become a "partaker of the divine nature," member of Christ and co-heir with him, and a temple of the Holy Spirit.

CCC 1266 The Most Holy Trinity gives the baptized sanctifying grace, the grace of *justification*:

- enabling them to believe in God, to hope in him, and to love him through the theological virtues;
- giving them the power to live and act under the prompting of the Holy Spirit through the gifts of the Holy Spirit;
- allowing them to grow in goodness through the moral virtues.

Thus the whole organism of the Christian's supernatural life has its roots in Baptism.

CCC 1294 Anointing with oil has all these meanings in the sacramental life. The pre-baptismal anointing with the oil of catechumens signifies cleansing and strengthening; the anointing of the sick expresses healing and comfort. The post-baptismal anointing with sacred chrism in Confirmation and ordination is the sign of consecration. By Confirmation Christians, that is, those who are anointed, share more completely in the mission of Jesus Christ and the fullness of the Holy Spirit with which he is filled, so that their lives may give off "the aroma of Christ."

CCC 1295 By this anointing the confirmand receives the "mark," the *seal* of the Holy Spirit. A seal is a symbol of a person, a sign of personal authority, or ownership of an object. Hence soldiers were marked with their leader's seal and slaves with their master's. A seal authenticates a juridical act or document and occasionally makes it secret.

CCC 1296 Christ himself declared that he was marked with his Father's seal. Christians are also marked with a seal: "It is God who establishes us with you in Christ and has commissioned us; he has put his seal on us and given us his Spirit in our hearts as a guarantee." This seal of the Holy Spirit marks our total belonging to Christ, our enrollment in his service for ever, as well as the promise of divine protection in the great eschatological trial.

CCC 1695 "Justified in the name of the Lord Jesus Christ and in the Spirit of our God," "sanctified . . . [and] called to be saints," Christians have become the temple of the Holy Spirit. This "Spirit of the Son" teaches them to pray to the Father and, having become their life, prompts them to act so as to bear "the fruit of the Spirit" by charity in action. Healing the wounds of sin, the Holy Spirit renews us interiorly through a spiritual transformation. He enlightens and strengthens us to live as "children of light" through "all that is good and right and true."

Verse Study

See Appendix 3 for instructions on how to complete a verse study.

John 10:9

1. Verse:

2. Paraphrase:

3. Questions:

4. Cross-references:

5. Personal Application:

Lesson 4

A MEDLEY OF PSALMS

Introduction

Sometimes we think that we have to get all cleaned up in order to come to God in prayer. And so, in times of weakness, stress, and struggle, we turn away from Him and look for help in other places. During these times God waits for us; He won't force His help on us. This means that we can end up missing out on power and strength that was ours for the taking. God wants us to turn immediately to Him, never hesitating for even a second. When we turn to Him "as is," He gives us the strength, virtue, and peace that we need. A study of Psalms reveals beautiful examples of the way we can approach God exactly as we are, exactly as we feel.

Approaching God authentically (i.e., in the moment just as we are, just as we feel) can be an act of worship. In coming to Him with bold honesty, we are acknowledging that He is big enough and strong enough to handle our emotions. We are turning to Christ as the Savior, rather than to some person or some other worldly thing that might give temporary comfort. Even when we turn to God with hearts that have a mix of emotions (love, fear, doubt), it is a recognition that God is greater than we are and that He offers something we lack.

How far can we go with what we say to God? Is there a point where we have moved from an honest expression of our feelings to a disrespect for Him that is actually a sin against His love? Honest prayers and questions are acceptable, but charging God with wrongdoing is a sin. According to CCC 2094, we sin against God's love through indifference or ingratitude, or when we're lukewarm.

If we are lukewarm with God, taking our passion and need elsewhere, we cause Him pain. We may feel that no one understands us the way a friend, parent, or spouse does, but the truth is, no one knows us better than Jesus. We learned in our lesson on Joseph, "For we have not a high priest [Jesus] who is unable to sympathize with our weaknesses, but one who in every respect has been tempted as we are, yet without sinning" (Hebrews 4:15). God wants us to worship Him with our whole hearts. He wants us to tell Him of our pain and distress. It's so easy to fall into gossip, sharing details of our situation with someone who isn't involved in the original problem or the solution. Why do we do it? We just have to get it out! We feel like we'll explode if we keep it all pent up inside. We just need to get it off our chests. God gets that. He opens His arms wide to us, His precious, precious daughters, and says, "Come to me! Trust me with your heart, with your hurt, with everything." We've got permission to let it all out. He can handle it. Our fiery female emotions don't hurt Him; our indifference does.

The Psalms give us wonderful examples of how to approach God honestly, but with a respect rooted in an understanding of His goodness, faithfulness, and greatness. Where do we go when our hearts are heavy with emotion, need, and problems? We go to Christ. He is the One who understands the emotion—after all, He created us. Only He can meet the need and handle the problem.

> Cry aloud to the Lord!
> O daughter of Zion!
> Let tears stream down like a torrent
> day and night!
> Give yourself no rest,
> your eyes no respite!
> Arise, cry out in the night,
> at the beginning of the watches!
> Pour out your heart like water
> before the presence of the Lord!
> Lift your hands to him
> for the lives of your children,
> who faint from hunger
> at the head of every street.
> (Lamentations 2:18–19)

Day One: Feeling Envious?

Read Psalm 37:1–7.

1. What is envy and what does the Bible have to say about it? See Psalm 37:1, 1 Peter 2:1, and CCC 2539.

2. So what do we do when we feel envious? We turn *to* God, not *away* from Him. Practically speaking, we stop the runaway freight train of our envious thoughts that lead us farther and farther from Christ, and we pray instead. We open our Bibles to Psalm 37 and begin reading. Tucked in verses 3 and 4 are instructions regarding what we should do instead of being envious. Write down those instructions, along with the promise made to us if we obey.

Verse 3
Instead of being envious, I will _____.

If I do this, I am promised _____.

Verse 4
Instead of being envious, I will _____.

If I do this, I am promised _____.

What is happening when we give in to envy? We aren't trusting God. In fact, we are really thinking that God is holding out on us. He's giving the good things to someone else and giving us the leftovers. This usually leads to self-pity. Feeling sorry for ourselves doesn't exactly motivate us to think of helping others and "doing good." But if we'll turn to God instead of away from Him, and recount the many times that He has proven to us just how trustworthy He is, we're promised that we can enjoy security. This true security isn't found in comfort, popularity, things, or achievements. It comes from knowing that our needs and deepest desires are met in Christ, and Christ alone.

Verse 4 highlights something else that happens when we give in to envy: We find our delight in something other than God. Whatever that something is, it will never satisfy us the way God does. Our hearts are easily fooled into thinking that whatever seems out of reach is exactly what would bring us the happiness we so desire. We need God to help us long for the right things. When someone has something or someone that you wish you had, say to the Lord, "God, open my eyes to see all the wonderful and satisfying things that are found in You. Help me to grow in my appreciation for all that You have given me! Renew a joy in my heart for the salvation You purchased for me at such a great cost." When we do this, we are delighting in God. He promises then that He'll give us the desires of our hearts. But an interesting thing has happened in the process: What we desire has changed. We have grown and now we want what He wants, which is always what's best for us.

3. In Psalm 37:5, we are told to commit our way to the Lord, to trust in Him, and then He will act. When He acts, what will He do? See Psalm 37:6.

4. In what way did the sin of envy impact Jesus during His time on earth? See Matthew 27:18.

Quiet your heart and enjoy His presence. . . . He alone truly satisfies.

How did the disciples feel when they were facing crowds of hungry people in John 6? The people had been listening to Jesus and had nowhere to go for dinner. They took a tally of what they had (five loaves of bread and two fish), and concluded that it was not enough. It wasn't enough to satisfy the hunger of each of them individually, and it wasn't enough for the crowd. Jesus asked them to give what they had to Him, and then He miraculously multiplied it. And everyone was satisfied. There were twelve baskets leftover—one for each disciple who had doubted that there would be enough.

When we struggle with envy, we're making the mistake of thinking that there is not enough in our lives to truly satisfy us. Jesus says the same thing to us that He said to the little boy with the loaves and fish: "Give me what you have." When we do, He multiplies our meager offering and proves that He is enough.

Dear Lord,

Please forgive me for wanting the gifts more than the Giver. Cleanse my heart so I want the things that You want. Help me to desire holiness more than anything. Restore to me the joy that comes from looking with a heart full of wonder at all You've promised and given me.

Day Two
FEELING BETRAYED?

Read Psalm 41:6–10.

1. Paraphrase the heartache of the psalmist that is recorded in Psalm 41:6–10.

2. In what way did Jesus experience the betrayal described in Psalm 41:10 (NAB)? See Mark 14:18–20.

3. Have you experienced betrayal at the hands of a friend? How did you respond? If you have experienced healing, what brought that about?

4. "All who hate me whisper together about me; they imagine the worst for me" (Psalm 41:7). Sometimes betrayal is a life-altering event. Other times it's the feeling of hurt that comes from someone simply imagining the worst about us. When our motives are misinterpreted, or when people make assumptions about us and think the worst of us when they don't have all the facts, it hurts! Has this ever been your experience? Explain.

5. Can you think of examples of times when we treat God in the same way described in Question 4? Is there a period in your own life when you have imagined the worst about God in the face of suffering? Time and time again in Scripture God assures us of His love and that He is *for us*. Yet how often do we struggle to trust Him? Might this be a subtle form of betrayal in a friendship? Discuss why or why not.

Quiet your heart and enjoy His presence. . . . Let nothing get between you and God.

When you've experienced the sting of betrayal, it's important to remember who the real enemy is: Satan. It isn't the friend who gossiped about you. It isn't the spouse who was unfaithful. It isn't the person who damaged your career path. Regardless of how much you may feel God has let you down, it isn't Him, either.

Satan, your real enemy, hates you. He doesn't just get annoyed by you. He despises you. Why? Because you are God's delight, His treasure. Satan knows he's no match for God, so he goes after His children instead. The enemy of your soul knows that "he who touches you touches the apple of [God's] eye" (Zechariah 2:8).

Satan does all he can to spread division. You can be assured that the discord you experience in relationships has been stoked and stirred by him. When you give in to bitterness, when you refuse to forgive, when you allow your hurt to drive a wedge between you and God, then you are handing Satan the victory. Hasn't he done enough damage? How would you like to put a stop to his divisive, destructive work?

One way to stop him in his tracks is to repent of anytime that you haven't given God the benefit of the doubt. Is there a time (perhaps even now) when you have assumed that the suffering He's allowed is for your harm? Have you attributed ill motive to the One who loves you like no other? Take some time to confess this and experience the freedom that comes from resting in the security of God's love.

Perhaps the enemy has been playing around with a relationship in your life. Are you the one who has been betrayed? Where should you begin in order to get out of Satan's messy web? You begin in the same way that the psalmist did in Psalm 41. In verse 4, he wrote, "O Lord, be gracious to me; heal me, for I have sinned against you!" He turned to God with his hurt instead of away from Him. He asked God to take note of him—to see him and his situation—and to respond with mercy and compassion. This is a request God always loves to answer with a resounding, "Yes, of course!"

This is an essential starting point if we're going to let go of hurt and be set free from the bitterness of unforgiveness. We must start with an awareness of our own propensity to mess up and our history of falling short. We may not have failed so terribly in terms of our relationship with the person who has hurt us, but we can certainly find evidence of times when we have been less than faithful to God. Yet how does He respond to us? With mercy, compassion, and forgiveness.

We alone can't free ourselves from unforgiveness. We need God's help. We can echo the words of Psalm 41:13: "You have upheld me because of my integrity, and set me in your presence for ever." Forgiving doesn't mean that we throw common sense out the door and continue in a relationship that is unhealthy. It doesn't mean enabling. We can forgive and still set boundaries. Forgiveness also doesn't let the other person off the hook with God. God will deal with the person who has hurt us. But when we forgive, we let go of the right to be the enforcer. If a punishment needs to be given, we trust it'll be given by God.

Is there a betrayal that you need to let go of? Are you feeling a tug on your heart to release this to God? Don't be afraid. Give it over to the One who loves you and wants to defend you. Let Him fight your battle. Spend some time in prayer, unclenching your fists and letting God have the hurt. Then ask Him to cover you with the balm of His love.

Day Three
FEELING GUILTY?

Have you ever felt that you can't get away from your sin? That even after saying you're sorry, the guilt feels like an oil that won't wash away? The words of Psalm 51 provide helpful steps to follow when we have messed up and desperately need a fresh start. This psalm was written by King David after he had an affair with a married woman and then had her husband killed in an attempt to cover his tracks. It provides an example of how to grieve over sin, what to do with feelings of guilt, and how to regret our actions well.

Read Psalm 51.

1. What is the first thing that David did in Psalm 51:3 (NAB)?

2. What was David's next step, seen in Psalm 51:4, 7 (NAB)?

David asked that God would cleanse him with hyssop, a plant with small, woody branches that was used in key moments in the salvation story. In Exodus 12:22, the Israelites were instructed to take a bunch of hyssop, dip it in the blood of the Passover lamb, and use it to apply the blood to the doorframe. The final plague would sweep through Egypt that night, and the firstborn in each house would be killed. But God would pass over the houses that had the blood on the door. The hyssop, the blood, and the sacrificed lamb would call down His mercy. In the New Testament, another Lamb was sacrificed: Jesus Christ. As His blood poured out, again God's mercy was called down. Jesus wanted God's judgment to "pass over" each one of us. But this mercy would come at a cost. As Jesus the Lamb bled on the cross, He said, "I thirst." "A bowl full of vinegar stood there; so they put a sponge full of the vinegar on hyssop and held it to his mouth" (John 19:29). The hyssop branch brought comfort to the Lamb as He died in our place.

When David confessed his sin, God passed over it. Does this mean that God didn't take seriously what David had done? No. God was looking ahead to the day when His Son, the Lamb of God, would die in David's place. David didn't "get away with" his sin. Someone paid the price, but it wasn't David. Jesus' sacrificial death on the cross paid the price for our sins. And because of this, God continues to "pass over" our sin today. He considers Christ's death on the cross the divine exchange—when Christ took our sins upon Himself and purchased our salvation with His righteousness. "For our sake he made him to be sin who knew no sin, so that in him we might become the righteousness of God" (2 Corinthians 5:21).

3. This life-giving grace cost Jesus everything He had. This is what we should focus on when we confess our sin. David took his sin seriously, providing an example for us to follow. List phrases in Psalm 51 that illustrate how seriously he took his sin.

4. The final way that David responded to his sin is found in Psalm 51:12 (NAB). Put his plea in your own words. Why do you think this final step is an essential part of dealing with guilt?

What steps did David take as he dealt with his guilt in Psalm 51? He turned to God, confessed his sin, took seriously its cost and consequence, and finally asked Him to renew his heart and change it from within. When we follow his example, our sin is forgiven. "He does not deal with us according to our sins, nor repay us according to our iniquities. For as the heavens are high above the earth, so great is his mercy towards those who fear him; as far as the east is from the west, so far does he remove our transgressions from us" (Psalm 103:10–12).

5. In spite of the assurance given in Psalm 103:10–12, for many of us, the guilt lingers, because we are struggling to forgive ourselves. What insight do we gain into this difficulty from Romans 8:1 and 1 John 3:19–20?

Quiet your heart and enjoy His presence. . . . Let Him lift the weight of guilt off your shoulders.

"The sacrifice acceptable to God is a broken spirit; a broken and contrite heart, O God, you will not despise" (Psalm 51:17). For us, as God's beloved daughters, a distinguishing characteristic should be our broken and contrite hearts. This is different from a heart that's weighed down with guilt. It's the heart of a woman who knows that apart from God, she is without hope. But she also knows that with Christ, all things are possible. This humility of heart is the best defense against a proud heart, which invariably leads to a fall. When a woman remains in this posture of brokenness before God, He will raise her up and use her in a mighty way in His kingdom. He isn't looking for the most popular, powerful, intelligent, or beautiful woman. He's looking for the woman who knows how much she needs Him.

Day Four
FEELING DESPONDENT?

Read Psalm 73:21–26.

1. What do you think the psalmist was experiencing in Psalm 73:26 when he wrote, "my flesh and my heart may fail"?

2. Has this ever been your experience? Can you share a time when a voice in your head whispered, "It won't work. There's no point in pressing on anymore"? Have your flesh and heart failed, making you want to give up? What is it that most often threatens your ability to persevere?

3. When our flesh and heart fail, feelings of despondency threaten to rob us of peace. We might feel we are sinking in a quagmire of circumstances and feelings, and can't seem to find our footing. When this is the case, we need to turn to Psalm 73:26, and rely on the promise contained in the second part of the verse: "God is the strength of my heart and my portion for ever." Write these words below, reflecting on why these truths make a difference in the face of despondency.

4. What similarities do you see in the psalmist's experience described in Psalm 73:21–26 and Jesus in the Garden of Gethsemane? See Matthew 26:36–46.

5. The choices Jesus made in the Garden of Gethsemane can guide us when we fight our own battles of despondency. Reflect back on your answer to Question 2. Matthew 26:36–46 describes Jesus in the pit of despair and sets forth the steps He took in the face of that despair. In the space provided after each verse, list a practical step you can take when you are experiencing this spiritual battle.

Verse 37: Jesus didn't battle alone. He asked a few trusted friends to stay with Him.

Verse 38: Jesus opened up and shared with His friends what He was feeling: "My soul is sorrowful, even to death."

Verse 39: Jesus employed the spiritual weapon of prayer.

Verse 41: Jesus asked His friends to pray for Him.

Verse 42: Jesus submitted His will to the Father's, and His heart found rest and peace even though His circumstances were unchanged.

Quiet your heart and enjoy His presence. . . . His strength is made perfect in your weakness.

Meditate on the following reflection on spiritual combat by Father Jacques Philippe. Choose one of the Bible verses in it to memorize, embrace, and remember as a promise and a spiritual truth from God's Word, which you can cling to in times of despondency. Let this verse be the sword of the Spirit that you wield in the face of discouragement and temptation to despair.

> *If the spiritual combat of a Christian is sometimes rough, it is by no means the hopeless struggle of somebody who battles in blindness and solitude, without any certitude as to the result of this confrontation. Rather, it is the combat of one who struggles with the absolute certitude that the victory is already won, because the Lord is resurrected.*

"... Do not weep. The lion of the tribe of Judah, the root of David, has triumphed, enabling him to open the scroll with its seven seals." (Revelation 5:5). He does not fight with his own strength, but with that of the Lord, Who says to him, "... My grace is sufficient for you, for power is made perfect in weakness." (2 Corinthians 12:9) and his principal weapon is not a natural firmness of character or human ability, but faith, this total adhesion to Christ which permits him, even in the worst moments, to abandon himself with a blind confidence in the One Who cannot abandon him. "I have the strength for everything through [God] who empowers me." (Philippians 4:13). "The Lord is my light and my salvation; whom do I fear?" (Psalm 27:1).*

"In your struggle against sin you have not yet resisted to the point of shedding blood." (Hebrews 12:4), but he fights with a peaceful heart and his struggle is that much more efficacious, because his heart is more peaceful. For, as we have said, it is exactly this interior peace which permits him to fight, not with his own strength, which would be quickly exhausted, but with the strength of God.[17]

Day Five
FEELING JOY?

Read Psalm 126.

Background information for Psalm 126: Because of their faithlessness, God had allowed the Israelites to be conquered by the Babylonians. They lived in captivity, exiled from the Promised Land. This not only took them from the security and comfort of their homes; it separated them from the temple, their means of drawing close to God and worshipping Him. After about fifty years of the Israelites' captivity, Cyrus, King of Persia, gave them permission to return to Jerusalem. Psalm 126 is the outpouring of joy from the hearts of the Jewish exiles who were allowed to come home.

1. What phrases in Psalm 126 reveal deep joy?

---

[17] Father Jacques Philippe, *Searching for and Maintaining Peace* (Staten Island, NY: Society of St. Paul, 2002), 9–10.

A Medley of Psalms | 4

2. Have you ever been so filled with joy that you thought you were dreaming? Share a story of a time when the Lord did something great for you.

3. What was the specific reason for the people's joy in Psalm 126? See verses 1 and 4.

4. What role did joy play in the life of Christ when He suffered on the cross? See Hebrews 12:2 and Acts 2:25–28.

5. What mission filled Jesus with joy during His time on earth? See Luke 4:18–19.

Quiet your heart and enjoy His presence. . . . He delights in you.

Never think that God is indifferent when you open your Bible to study His Word. He doesn't approach you nonchalantly when you ask Him for His mercy in confession. He is not unmoved when you surrender your will to His. When you turn to Him, He is like the father in the parable of the prodigal son—running to you, ready to throw a party, filled with joy over you! When we wander away into places of captivity, condemnation, or despair, God longs for us to return to Him and walk in the freedom He offers. His heart is reflected in the parable of the lost sheep. "What man of you," Jesus said, "having a hundred sheep, if he has lost one of them, does not leave the ninety-nine in the wilderness, and go after the one which is lost, until he finds it? And when he has found it, he lays it on his shoulders, rejoicing. And when he comes home, he calls together his friends and his neighbors, saying to them, 'Rejoice with me, for I have found my sheep which was lost.' Just so, I tell you, there will be more joy in heaven over one sinner who repents than over ninety-nine righteous persons who need no repentance" (Luke 15:4–7).

You bring Him joy and delight. Whenever you turn to Him, you console His heart. You don't have to talk to Him with fancy words. You don't have to put on a show and impress Him with all you know. He just wants you to turn your eyes and heart to Him. Let the things that distract and worry you fade away as you focus on the One who has set you free. Joy!

Conclusion

I encourage you to mark up your Bible with your story. Write the emotions highlighted in this lesson (envy, betrayal, guilt, despondency, joy) next to the psalm that addresses them. When other verses in Scripture speak to you, underline them and write a little note and date there. Your life is a beautiful tapestry, woven by God. Along the journey, there are periods of pain, fear, and joy. At each point, God is teaching you something. He is always speaking to us through Scripture. When we've recorded those lessons, we can go back to them later and be assured that He is faithful.

God has given us the Psalms to help us express our emotions in a way that draws us *to* Him, not *away* from Him. When we linger and dwell in the Psalms, we find comfort in the saints who have gone before us. They faced the same sorrows and joys that we face, and their sorrows and joys led them to focus on God's goodness, faithfulness, and promised rescue.

How fortunate we are that we know the end of the story! The psalmists wrote of a future hope, based solely on God's promises. We *know* that future hope: Christ. *We can see how all the promises have been fulfilled in Him!*

David pleaded with God, "Cast me not away from your presence, and take not your holy Spirit from me" (Psalm 51:11). What a privilege it is that we can come face-to-face with God. What intimacy He offers us in the Eucharist, in the confessional, in adoration. But He doesn't stop there. He has placed His Holy Spirit into our hearts, so that no matter where we are, we can turn our faces to His and receive His mercy and love.

My Resolution

In what specific way will I apply what I learned in this lesson?

Examples:

1. In order to renew my mind—asking for the mind of Christ instead of being ruled by my emotions—I will read one psalm and one proverb every day of the week. If it is the 12th of the month, I'll read the 12th Psalm and Proverbs 12. If it's the 23rd of the month, I'll read the 23rd Psalm and Proverbs 23.

2. Each night before sleeping, I'll count my blessings. I'll focus on the joy that is mine because of the freedom I've been given in Christ. I'll count the ways in which God has poured out undeserved kindness on me throughout the day.

3. When I confess my sins, I'll pay special attention to the subtle sin of envy. Have I been focusing on what I don't have, and those who have what I want? I'll confess this as a lack of trust in God, who gives me everything that I need. "His divine power has bestowed on us everything that makes for life and devotion" (2 Peter 1:3).

My resolution:

Catechism Clips

CCC 1850 Sin is an offense against God: "Against you, you alone, have I sinned, and done that which is evil in your sight." Sin sets itself against God's love for us and turns our hearts away from it. Like the first sin, it is disobedience, a revolt against God through the will to become "like gods," knowing and determining good and evil. Sin is thus "love of oneself even to contempt of God." In this proud self-exaltation, sin is diametrically opposed to the obedience of Jesus, which achieves our salvation.

CCC 2539 Envy is a capital sin. It refers to the sadness at the sight of another's goods and the immoderate desire to acquire them for oneself, even unjustly. When it wishes grave harm to a neighbor it is a mortal sin:

> St. Augustine saw envy as "*the* diabolical sin." "From envy are born hatred, detraction, calumny, joy caused by the misfortune of a neighbor, and displeasure caused by his prosperity."

A Medley of Psalms | 4

Verse Study

See Appendix 3 for instructions on how to complete a verse study.

Psalm 19:8–9

1. Verse:

2. Paraphrase:

3. Questions:

4. Cross-references:

5. Personal Application:

SOLOMON'S TEMPLE AND THE DIVIDED KINGDOM

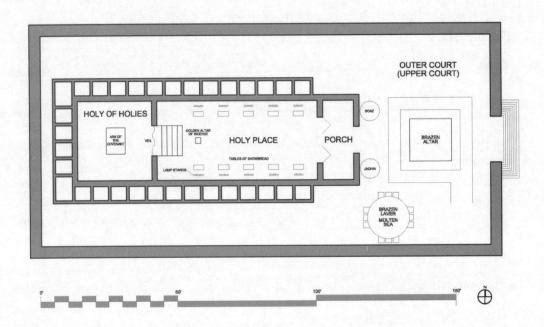

Lesson 5: Connect Coffee Talk 2
THE TEMPLE – I INVITE YOU IN

Accompanying talk can be viewed by DVD or digital download purchase or access online at walkingwithpurpose.com/videos.

1. **The Old Way to Approach God**

    In Leviticus 17:11, God said, "the life of the flesh is in the _____, and I have given it to you to make atonement on the altar for yourselves, because it is the blood . . . that makes atonement."

    Hebrews 9:22: "According to the law almost everything is purified by _____, and without the shedding of _____ there is no forgiveness."

    Only one person was allowed to enter the Holy of Holies: the _____.

    He was allowed to enter _____ a year, on Yom Kippur, the day of _____.

    Hebrews 9:6

2. **The New and Living Way to Access God**

    Matthew 27:50

Hebrews 10:19

Hebrews 10:1

Hebrews 9:12

Romans 5:8–9: "But God proves his love for us in that while we were still sinners Christ died for us. How much more then, since we are now _____ by his _____, we will be saved through him from the wrath."

Romans 5:1–2: "Therefore, since we have been justified by faith, we have peace with God through our Lord Jesus Christ, through whom we have _____ _____ to this grace in which we stand."

3. The Difference It Makes to Be Family

John 1:12

Ephesians 2:13

Hebrews 10:19–22

Questions for Discussion

1. In the Old Testament, women had no access to God. They could know Him from a distance, but they could not draw near. Can you think of things that cause women today to feel that they aren't good enough to draw near to God? Have you ever experienced this personally? Share your story.

2. We aren't shut out from God's presence by a thick curtain. We aren't put on hold and told to wait an indefinite amount of time. Why? Because we are family. What does it mean to you to be God's daughter?

3. In the words of Ann Voskamp, "He has touched our tears. He has cupped our broken hearts with His scars. He has whispered to the howl, 'I know, I know. And I've come to begin the making of all things new."[18] What is causing your heart to feel broken right now? In what area of your life do you need Jesus to come and make all things new?

---

[18] Ann Voskamp, "When You're Struggling Through Holy Week (Thursday)," A Holy Experience, March 28, 2013, http://www.aholyexperience.com/2013/03/when-youre-struggling-through-holy-week-thursday/.

NOTES

Walking with Purpose is a community of women growing in faith – together! This is where women are gathering. Join us!

www.walkingwithpurpose.com

Lesson 6
ISAIAH 53

Introduction

Have you ever had an experience that changed the direction of your life? Perhaps it was the birth of a child, or a trauma, or a moment of pure inspiration that unleashed a passion. The prophet Isaiah described that juncture in his life in the following way: "In the year that King Uzziah died I saw the Lord" (Isaiah 6:1). He saw the Lord, and his life was changed. This vision of God in His glory, seated on a lofty throne, so filled Isaiah's heart and mind that he was never the same again.

Isaiah devoted his life to speaking the truth that God revealed to him. When he spoke, his words flew like arrows into the hearts of his listeners. Sometimes they were words of comfort that were well received. More often, they were words of reproach and condemnation in response to the Israelite people's disobedience to God. These confrontations didn't make the prophet very popular.

Popularity wasn't Isaiah's goal. His vision of God propelled him into ministry, and kept him faithful. Regardless of how he was received, he begged his people to rely on God instead of placing their security in alliances with pagan nations. This call to holiness went beyond encouraging good outward behavior. Isaiah knew that God was concerned with the state of the heart.

Being God's voice to a rebellious people must have been a lonely job. How often did the Old Testament prophets wonder if it would ever get better? God knew just when the prophets and His people needed hope. Threaded throughout the Old Testament, and many times in the book of Isaiah, are prophecies about Jesus. These prophecies served multiple purposes. They reminded the people of that day when a rescuer was coming, they motivated the prophets to keep serving the One who holds all of history and the future in His hands, and they confirm to us today that God's plans will come to pass, down to the tiniest detail.

Here are some of the prophecies found in Isaiah:

Isaiah 7:14: "Therefore the Lord himself will give you a sign. Behold, a virgin shall conceive and bear a son, and shall call his name Imman´u-el."

Isaiah 9:6–7: "For to us a child is born, to us a son is given; and the government will be upon his shoulder, and his name will be called 'Wonderful Counselor, Mighty God, Everlasting Father, Prince of Peace.' Of the increase of his government and of peace there will be no end, upon the throne of David, and over his kingdom, to establish it, and to uphold it with justice and righteousness from this time forth and for evermore"

Isaiah 35:4–6: "Say to those who are of a fearful heart, 'Be strong, fear not! Behold, your God will come with vengeance, with the recompense of God. He will come and save you.' Then the eyes of the blind shall be opened, and the ears of the deaf unstopped; then shall the lame man leap like a deer, and the tongue of the mute sing for joy."

Isaiah 40:1–5, 9–11: "Comfort, comfort my people, says your God. Speak tenderly to Jerusalem, and cry to her that her warfare has ended, that her iniquity is pardoned, that she has received from the Lord's hand double for all her sins. A voice cries: In the wilderness prepare the way of the LORD, make straight in the desert a highway for our God. Every valley shall be lifted up, and every mountain and hill be made low; the uneven ground shall become level, and the rough places a plain. And the glory of the LORD shall be revealed, and all flesh shall see it together . . . Get you up to a high mountain, O Zion, herald of good tidings; lift up your voice with strength, O Jerusalem, herald of good tidings, lift it up, fear not; say to the cities of Judah, 'Behold your God!' Behold, the Lord God comes with might and his arm rules for him; behold, his reward is with him, and his recompense before him. He will feed his flock like a shepherd, he will gather the lambs in his arms, he will carry them in his bosom, and gently lead those that are with young."

Isaiah 50:6: "I gave my back to those who struck me, and my cheeks to those who pulled out the beard; I hid not my face from shame and spitting."

Perhaps no chapter of Isaiah points more completely to Jesus than Isaiah 53. As you study, don't lose the wonder of the fact that these things were written seven hundred years before Christ walked the earth. God's plan was in place long before it was seen on earth. His plan for your life is no different. Even if evidence suggests otherwise, there is nothing in your life that is not under His control. He's got it. And He's bringing all the threads of your life—no matter how shredded they may feel—and creating a beautiful tapestry. He can take anything and weave it into His perfect plan.

Isaiah 53 | 6

Day One
WHAT MORE COULD JESUS DO TO HELP YOU BELIEVE?

Read Isaiah 53, paying special attention to verses 1–3.

1. Isaiah's words in verse 1 describe the disbelief and resistance he encountered when he preached to the Israelites. A form of the Hebrew word *zeroa*, translated "arm" in Isaiah 53, is used elsewhere in Scripture to describe the strength and power of God's works. Reflect back on Lesson 7 (Moses) in the Bible study that preceded this one, *Beholding His Glory*. What examples do you see of God's arm giving evidence of the strength and power of His works? List ways in which "the arm of the Lord [had] been revealed" to the Israelites. What should the result have been when they witnessed His arm at work? See Exodus 6:6 and Deuteronomy 4:34.

2. In what way were Isaiah's words in Isaiah 53:1 also a prophecy to be fulfilled seven hundred years later? See John 12:37–38 and Romans 10:16.

3. "Jesus asked the religious authorities of Jerusalem to believe in him because of the Father's works which he accomplished" (CCC 591). What insight do we gain from CCC 591 regarding the reason why it was so hard for the Jewish people of Jesus' day to believe in Him? Do you think this is the same reason it's so hard for people *today* to believe in Jesus?

4. Recalling Day Four of Lesson 2 (David), what is the significance of the imagery of a sapling and a shoot in Isaiah 53:2? See also Isaiah 11:1 and 11:10.

5. Describe how the verses of Isaiah 53:2–3 are a description of Jesus.

Quiet your heart and enjoy His presence. . . . Let Him bring you close and closer still.

We're sometimes hard on the religious authorities of Jesus' time, shaking our heads at their rejection of the One who had come to save them all. But when we think about their unmet expectations, we can't help but realize that we, too, come to Jesus with expectations. When those expectations aren't met, we're tempted to turn our faces away from Him, to spurn Him, to hold Him in low esteem.

Isaiah tells us, "He had no form or comeliness that we should look at him, and no beauty that we should desire him" (Isaiah 53:2). Perhaps this was so that the heart could draw, instead of the physical appearance. What draws you to Jesus? Resist the temptation to just read that question and move on; instead, take a moment to really think about your answer. God could have created us so that loving Him was not a choice but an automatic response. But this wasn't what He wanted. He wanted a genuine relationship with His children, based on our free decision to embrace Him. He could have bribed us by always giving us whatever we want. But again, He wanted a true love, based on who He is, not what He gives.

He wants us to be drawn to Him because of His merciful, selfless, sacred heart. Can you praise Him today for who He is? Find the Litany of Praise in the appendix, and spend some time telling your Savior how special He is to you.

Day Two
ALL FOR LOVE OF YOU

Read Isaiah 53:4–6.

1. When was the last time you or a loved one experienced something that was unfair? How might Isaiah 53:4–6 be rewritten if life were fair?

2. "He was . . . bruised for our iniquities" (Isaiah 53:5). The Hebrew word translated as "bruised" is *daka*, meaning "broken into pieces, shattered." Often when this word is used in Scripture, it's describing emotional or spiritual anguish rather than a physical bruising. In what way would this be true of Jesus' experience? See 2 Corinthians 5:21.

3. "And with his stripes we are healed" (Isaiah 53:5).

    A. What were the physical wounds that Christ suffered? What image does the word "stripes" bring to mind when you think of Jesus' passion? See Mark 15:15, 17 and John 19:18, 34.

    B. A day is coming when the One who was pierced for our sins will return. According to Revelation 1:7, who will see Christ at His second coming?

4. According to Isaiah 53:6, Romans 3:23, and 1 John 1:8, who has gone astray? Who is in need of healing from sin? How do you think the mainstream culture would answer this question?

Isaiah 53 | 6

5. Why did Jesus endure the physical and emotional pain of the crucifixion? See Isaiah 53:5.

Quiet your heart and enjoy His presence. . . . Let Him heal your heart.

Jesus endured the agony of the cross because He desperately wanted to see you whole and healed. The highest priority for Him is to see you healed from the effects of sin. He knows that He is the only answer—only He can stand in your place and bear the punishment. The first step to experience this healing is to admit that you need it. It's only when you throw yourself on His mercy that you can experience this healing. We have all gone astray like sheep, all following our own way. We've fallen, and we need the Good Shepherd to pick us up. He extends His arms, saying, "Please stop wandering. Come home, and let me heal you." Are you tired of wandering? Are you ready for rest? Lay down your sins at the foot of the cross. Ask Jesus to take them. See His wounds. Meditate on what it cost Jesus to offer you healing. Picture your sins placed on Him. Thank Him for stepping in front of the punishment that was due you and receiving it Himself. Then ask for His healing. He didn't die for you so that you could walk around the rest of your life with burdens, guilt, fear, and brokenness. He came to heal and restore you. Take His outstretched hand.

"Can a woman forget her sucking child, that she should have no compassion on the son of her womb? Even these may forget, yet I will not forget you. Behold, I have graven you on the palms of my hands" (Isaiah 49:15–16).

Day Three
GRACE IN THE FACE OF SUFFERING

Read Isaiah 53:7–9.

1. What were the two remarkable responses of the suffering Servant to the harsh treatment He received?

2. In what specific ways did Jesus fulfill Isaiah's prophecy by willingly submitting to His passion? See John 10:18 and Matthew 26:53–54.

3. At what points did Jesus fulfill Isaiah's prophecy by remaining silent in the face of harsh treatment and certain death? See Matthew 26:62–63 and 27:13–14, and Luke 23:8–9.

4. In Acts 8, an Ethiopian eunuch was sitting in his chariot, reading out loud from this passage of Isaiah: "As a sheep led to the slaughter or a lamb before its shearer is silent, so he opens not his mouth. In his humiliation justice was denied him. Who can describe his generation? For his life is taken up from the earth." Just at that point, Philip was passing by, and asked the man if he understood the passage. The eunuch begged Philip to explain, so Philip taught him who Jesus was and why He came to earth, based on this passage. The eunuch was baptized that very day. How would you explain who Jesus is and why He came to earth, using this passage as your starting point?

5. Isaiah 53:5–6 and 9 are quoted in 1 Peter to encourage Christians to follow Christ's example when enduring their own suffering. What practical application can you make from 1 Peter 2:21–25 regarding your own difficulties?

Quiet your heart and enjoy His presence. . . . Let the Holy Spirit strengthen you from within.

Is it possible that the difficulty you are facing today is actually an answer to one of your prayers? We pray that we would have humility, and God sends us opportunities to practice the virtue. We're misunderstood or falsely accused, or credit for something that we have done goes to another person. It's so hard to experience something unkind being said about us, and then respond with grace. But how we respond to situations like these exposes who we really are. To turn the other cheek takes the strength that was in Christ when He "though harshly treated . . . submitted and did not open his mouth" (NAB). The good news is, the Holy Spirit has been placed in our hearts to help us to do what we couldn't do without Him. We only need to ask, and He will give us what we need. "For because [Jesus] himself has suffered and been tempted, he is able to help those who are tempted" (Hebrews 2:18). Is there an area of your life that God is asking you to release to His care? Can you let Him be the judge? Can you respond with humility and grace? Take a few moments to ask the Holy Spirit to release in you the strength to respond as Jesus would.

Day Four
FOR HIS NAME'S SAKE

Read Isaiah 53:10.

Isaiah 53:10, "Yet it was the will of the Lord to bruise him," can be hard to understand. How do we reconcile a loving Father with a willingness to crush His Son with pain? Making sense of this passage requires a look at what gives God pleasure.

Throughout Scripture, God delights in seeing His name honored and glorified. When God spoke to Pharaoh in Egypt, He said, "But for this purpose have I let you live, to show you my power, so that *my name* may be declared throughout all the earth." (Exodus 9:16; emphasis added) God "saved [the Israelites] *for his name's sake*" (Psalm 106:8; emphasis added), and was their king, leading them from slavery in Egypt to freedom. Years after settling in the Promised Land, His people wanted to be like everyone else around them. They wanted a *human* king. This rejection of God's kingship over them could have caused the Lord to turn away from the Israelites, but instead, He inspired the prophet Samuel to tell them, "For the LORD will not cast away his people, *for his great name's sake*, because it pleased the LORD to make you a people for himself" (1 Samuel 12:22; emphasis added). God would not abandon His people—not because of their great loyalty and love for Him, but for the sake of His name. The phrase "for his great name's sake" can be understood as referring to God's reputation. Simply because He wanted to, God chose to tie His reputation, His name, to the destiny of His people.

God loves to see His name honored and glorified, especially when it is reflected in His children. Zephaniah 3:17 paints a beautiful picture of His delight in us: "The Lord, your God, is in your midst, a warrior who gives victory; he will rejoice over you with gladness, he will renew you in his love; he will exult over your with loud singing!" Nothing delights God more than when we reflect His glory to the world around us.

But there's a problem. Historically and in the present day, God's children often fail to reflect His glory. In fact, Romans 3:23 (RSV) sums it up: "All have sinned, and fall short of the glory of God." We could choose to live for God's glory, but all too often, we substitute His glory with something else (comfort, a good reputation, money, some item).

So how do we reconcile God having both pleasure in the glory of His own *good* name and pleasure in the people who often give Him a *bad* name? We find the resolution to this in Isaiah 53:10.

1. How was the prophet Isaiah describing Christ in the following phrases: "to bruise him," "he shall prolong his days," and "he shall see his offspring"?

2. "All we like sheep have gone astray; we have turned every one to his own way; and the LORD has laid on him the iniquity of us all" (Isaiah 53:6). Based on the introduction to today's questions, why couldn't God just ignore or gloss over "the iniquity of us all"?

3. In what way does Christ's death on the cross demonstrate to the world that God's glory matters?

4. How do we reconcile God having both pleasure in the glory of His own *good* name and pleasure in the people who often give Him a *bad* name? In other words, what makes up for our disobedience to God? See CCC 615.

5. We can respond to these truths by giving intellectual assent—a nod of the head and a cerebral appreciation that we don't have to pay the price for our sins. And as we wipe our foreheads in relief, we might even mistakenly feel the freedom to live however we'd like. What is Saint Paul's reaction to this response? He wrote, "What shall we say then? Are we to continue in sin that grace may abound? By no means!" (Romans 6:1) What should be our response to this gift of grace? See Romans 6:15–18.

Quiet your heart and enjoy His presence. . . . For the glory of His name.

God looks at you and whispers, "Display my glory to a world that is desperate to see something beautiful, something holy, something selfless, something authentic!" How will you respond?

Take some time to recount how God has touched your life— the times He has intervened and come through for you. When were you at the end of your rope but somehow managed to hold on? When did deliverance come when you were out of options? When were your prayers answered?

Then reflect back on moments of your life when things happened that were just delightful and good— the times you laughed or cried for joy, the times when you lost yourself in the moment because the reality of it was so special. Have you been moved by a beautiful piece of art? Or a stirring piece of music? Or a story that utterly transfixed you? God was orchestrating your times of joy, and seeing your smile gave Him such pleasure.

How can we be the same after being touched by God so personally?

May our hearts be grateful and faithful in response to Him. May we show Him our appreciation, not just with our words, but with our very lives. May we live out heroic virtue, love without counting the cost, turn the other cheek, and remain peaceful despite our circumstances. If we will do this, we'll bring glory to God's name.

Day Five
NOT GUILTY

Read Isaiah 53:11–12.

1. What will God's servant (the just One) do, according to Isaiah 53:11 (NAB)?

2. The verb *justify* means "to acquit," "to declare innocent." What additional understanding about being justified can be gained from CCC 1990?

3. What do we need to do if we are going to experience justification, according to CCC 1991, CCC 1992, and Romans 5:1?

4. In Romans 10:9–10, Saint Paul wrote, "If you confess with your lips that Jesus is Lord and believe in your heart that God raised him from the dead, you will be saved. For man believes with his heart and so is justified, and he confesses with his lips and so is saved." According to this verse, what part does the heart play in our justification? What do you think gets in the way of the spiritual truths we learn going from the head to the heart?

5. What does being declared "not guilty" mean to you personally?

Quiet your heart and enjoy His presence. . . . Believe with your heart that His love for you has no limit.

Jesus proved that His love for you has no limit when He "poured out his soul to death" (Isaiah 53:12) in your place. Take a moment to let that truth journey from your head to your heart.

How will you respond to His surrender? Can you allow it to draw you deeply into His love? Can you offer Him your heart in return? Surrendering to God in response to His limitless love is the key to living a life of freedom. The following prayer of surrender is taken from the booklet Miracle Hour: A Method of Prayer That Will Change Your Life. *If you are ready to take the journey from the head to the heart, these words will help you to offer the Lord what He deeply desires.*

A Prayer of Surrender

Loving Father, I surrender to You today with all my heart and soul. Please come into my heart in a deeper way. I say "yes," to You today. I open all the secret places of my heart to You and say, "Come on in." Jesus you are Lord of my whole life. I believe in You as my Lord and Savior. I hold nothing back. Holy Spirit, bring me to deeper conversion to the person of Jesus Christ. I surrender all to You: my health, my family, my resources, occupation, skills, relationships, time management, successes and failures. I release it, and let it go. I surrender my understanding of how things ought to be, my choices and my will. I surrender to You the promises I have kept and the promises I have failed to keep. I surrender my weaknesses and strengths to You. I surrender my emotions, my fears, my insecurities, my sexuality. I especially surrender _____, _____, _____. Lord, I surrender my entire life to You, the past, the present, and the future. In sickness and in health, in life and in death, I belong to You.[19]

Conclusion

"Yet it was the will of the Lord to bruise him" (Isaiah 53:10). With this verse, we are assured that when Jesus died on the cross, it wasn't evidence of God's loss of control. It wasn't the victory of evil over good. It was, in fact, the moment in history when God's incredible plan was accomplished through Jesus. Nothing took Him by surprise. Saint Peter spoke of this at Pentecost: "This Jesus, delivered up according to the definite plan and foreknowledge of God, you crucified and killed by the hands of lawless men. But God raised him up, having loosed the pangs of death, because it was not possible for him to be held by it" (Acts 2:23–24). It seemed like God's plan had gone awry. Yet that was exactly when the battle was won.

There was a battle, and there were spoils of war. This was spoken of in Isaiah 53:12: "I will divide him a portion with the great, and he shall divide the spoil with the strong; because he poured out his soul to death." The spoils of the battle are shared with us. Why? Because God knows that we are fighting in a battle, too. He knows there are times when it feels like all hope is lost, when it seems like evil is stronger than good. Author L. B. Cowman gives insight into what these spoils of battle are like and how we are to use them:

> The Gospel and the gift of God are structured so wonderfully that the very enemies and forces that are marshaled to fight against us actually help pave our

---

[19] Linda Schubert, *Miracle Hour: A Method of Prayer That Will Change Your Life,* (Santa Clara, CA: Miracles of the Heart Ministries, 1991), 12–13. Reprinted with Permission. http://www.linda-schubert.com/.

way to the very gates of heaven and into the presence of God. . . . He wants us to be "more than conquerors" . . . It is obvious when an army becomes "more than conquerors," for it drives its enemies from the battlefield and confiscates their food and supplies. . . . There are spoils to be taken!

Dear believer, after experiencing the terrible valley of suffering, did you depart with the spoils? When you were struck with an injury and you thought you had lost everything, did you trust in God to the point that you came out richer than you went in? Being "more than [a] conqueror" means taking the spoils from the enemy and appropriating them for yourself. What your enemy had planned to use for your defeat, you can confiscate for your own use.[20]

We can take the very things meant to destroy us and, with God's help, come out stronger, better, victorious!

My Resolution

In what specific way will I apply what I learned in this lesson?

Examples:

1. I'll pray the Litany of Praise (Appendix 6) every day this week to bring glory to God's name.

2. When I reflect on my current difficulties each day, I will check to see if there is any aspect of my circumstance that is actually an answer to prayer. Is this difficulty actually an opportunity for me to develop a desired virtue?

3. I will go to adoration and meditate on Christ's passion and death, thanking Him for what it cost Him to absolve me with the words "not guilty."

My resolution:

---

[20] L. B. Cowman, *Streams in the Desert* (Grand Rapids, MI: Zondervan, 2007), 469.

Catechism Clips

CCC 591 Jesus asked the religious authorities of Jerusalem to believe in him because of the Father's works which he accomplished. But such an act of faith must go through a mysterious death to self, for a new "birth from above" under the influence of divine grace. Such a demand for conversion in the face of so surprising a fulfillment of the promises allows one to understand the Sanhedrin's tragic misunderstanding of Jesus: they judged that he deserved the death sentence as a blasphemer. The members of the Sanhedrin were thus acting at the same time out of "ignorance" and the "hardness" of their "unbelief."

CCC 615 "For as by one man's disobedience many were made sinners, so by one man's obedience many will be made righteous." By his obedience unto death, Jesus accomplished the substitution of the suffering Servant, who "makes himself an *offering for sin*," when "he bore the sin of many," and who "shall make many to be accounted righteous," for "he shall bear their iniquities." Jesus atoned for our faults and made satisfaction for our sins to the Father.

CCC 1990 Justification *detaches man from sin* which contradicts the love of God, and purifies his heart of sin. Justification follows upon God's merciful initiative of offering forgiveness. It reconciles man with God. It frees from the enslavement to sin, and it heals.

CCC 1991 Justification is at the same time *the acceptance of God's righteousness* through faith in Jesus Christ. Righteousness (or "justice") here means the rectitude of divine love. With justification, faith, hope, and charity are poured into our hearts, and obedience to the divine will is granted us.

CCC 1992 Justification has been *merited for us by the Passion of Christ* who offered himself on the cross as a living victim, holy and pleasing to God, and whose blood has become the instrument of atonement for the sins of all men. Justification is conferred in Baptism, the sacrament of faith. It conforms us to the righteousness of God, who makes us inwardly just by the power of his mercy. Its purpose is the glory of God and of Christ, and the gift of eternal life:

> "But now the righteousness of God has been manifested apart from law, although the law and the prophets bear witness to it, the righteousness of God through faith in Jesus Christ for all who believe. For there is no distinction: since all have sinned and fall short of the glory of God, they are justified by his grace as a gift, through the redemption which is in Christ Jesus, whom God put forward as an expiation by his blood, to be received by faith. This was to show

God's righteousness, because in his divine forbearance he had passed over former sins; it was to prove at the present time that he himself is righteous and that he justifies him who has faith in Jesus." (Romans 3:21–26)

Verse Study

See Appendix 3 for instructions on how to complete a verse study.

Romans 5:17

1. Verse:

2. Paraphrase:

3. Questions:

4. Cross-references:

5. Personal Application:

Lesson 7

JEREMIAH AND EZEKIEL

Introduction

Throughout the Old Testament, God made promises to His people and always followed through on them. In the book of Genesis, His promises to Abraham were later raised to the status of a covenant. God promised:

1) to make Abraham a great nation (a promise of land)
2) to make his name great (a promise of a kingdom)
3) to bless the whole world through Abraham (a promise of a worldwide blessing)

Generations later, Moses led the Israelites (Abraham's descendants) out of slavery in Egypt. He went up Mount Sinai to pray, and received the following message from God: "Tell the sons of Israel: You have seen what I did the Egyptians, and how I bore you on eagles' wings and brought you to myself. Now, therefore, if you will obey my voice and keep my covenant, you shall be my own possession among all peoples; for all the earth is mine, and you shall be to me a kingdom of priests and a holy nation" (Exodus 19:3–6). God revealed His heart's desire—for the nation of Israel to be His treasured possession, a kingdom of priests, poised to show the world how wonderful it is to live under the shadow of God's wings. But it all depended on a very big "if." "**If** you will obey my voice and keep my covenant," God had said. Unfortunately, much of the Old Testament is the record of the many ways in which the Israelites failed to keep up their side of the covenant.

God sent prophets (Elijah, Elisha, Hosea, Isaiah, Jeremiah, Ezekiel, and many more) to point the Israelites toward holiness and away from sin. But time and time again, they chose to worship idols and other gods. What was the consequence of their rebellion? God allowed Assyria to conquer the Northern Kingdom (Israel) and Babylon to conquer the Southern Kingdom (Judah). This was the punishment for generations and centuries of sin.

Regardless of how far the Israelites fell, God never stopped loving them. He raised up prophets who spoke not only words of judgment but also words of hope—they told the Israelites that one day God would restore them and bring them home. Jeremiah and Ezekiel were two of those prophets sent to the Southern Kingdom. Jeremiah preached before the exile (although his writings were read throughout the exile) and Ezekiel preached during the exile, after the people of Judah were deported to Babylon.

The old covenant had been broken, but hope remained. Jeremiah and Ezekiel spoke to the heart of the matter, pointing forward to a day when a new covenant would come. This covenant would be unlike anything anyone had previously experienced. It would come at a cost, but would be for our eternal gain.

Note: For more explanation on the covenants, see Appendix 4: Covenants – God's Family Bond.

Day One
WHAT HAS TRUE WORTH

Read Jeremiah 2:1–13.

1. What did the prophet Jeremiah say that God had done for the Israelites? How had they responded?

2. God asked His people, "What wrong did your fathers find in me that they went far from me, and went after worthlessness, and became worthless?" (Jeremiah 2:5) There are many things in our current day that tempt us to withdraw from God and go after worthless things instead. Many of these patterns of behavior have been passed down from one generation to the next. Think of your family of origin and your ancestors. Are there any patterns of pursuing worthless things that you can see tracing back through your family line? Ask God to reveal them to you, and sit in quietness to listen. If you identify a generational sin (for example, alcoholism, greed, adultery, divorce, materialism, gluttony), write a prayer of confession and ask that the waters of your baptism would flow back through your ancestral line,

cleansing it of this sin. Ask God to break this chain of sin so that it will no longer lead you and future generations toward emptiness.

3. People rarely pursue worthless, empty things because they intentionally want to turn from or hurt God. More often, they thirst for significance and fulfillment. They just look in the wrong places. How is this process described in Jeremiah 2:13? Where is the best place to turn with our thirst for significance? See John 4:13–14.

4. A. If you could ask God for anything—if you could be guaranteed that one desire would be granted in your lifetime—what would you ask for? Write it below. Think about what you would be willing to do in order to see that desire actualized. Would you be willing to sell everything you had in order to gain it?

B. There had been a time when Israel's love for God delighted Him. God could "remember the devotion of [their] youth, [their] loved as a bride, how [they] followed [Him] in the wilderness, in a land not sown. Israel was holy to the Lord, the first fruits of his harvest" (Jeremiah 2:2–3). But something changed. Somewhere along the way, they started loving something else more than Him. We can relate to this. Rarely is this shift a *sudden* change. It's subtle. We don't immediately reject God; we just try to serve two masters. "No one can serve two masters; for either he will hate the one and love the other, or he will be devoted to the one and despise the other" (Matthew 6:24). What kind of focus do we need in order to keep our love for God alive? See Matthew 13:45–46.

5. According to the world's standards at that time, Saint Paul had it all. "Circumcised on the eighth day, of the people of Israel, of the tribe of Benjamin, a Hebrew born of Hebrews; as to the law a Pharisee, as to zeal a persecutor of the Church, as to righteousness under the law blameless" (Philippians 3:5–6). He had the breeding, reputation, education, and position that Jewish men of that time dreamed of. How did he measure the worth of all those things against knowing Christ? See Philippians 3:7–9.

Quiet your heart and enjoy His presence. . . . He's the pearl of great price.

"Worthy is the Lamb who was slain, to receive power and wealth and wisdom and might and honor and glory and blessing" (Revelation 5:12).

Lord, You are the matchless treasure. Nothing is worth more than You. Help me to see the ways in which my compromise comes at a cost. I long to have my emptiness filled, but so often compromise and try to fill it with things that don't really satisfy. There are so many things in my life that seem so important. I can focus on education, reputation, the development of talents, financial security, accomplishment of goals, parenting, marriage, career . . . These aren't harmful things, unless I put them before You. Help me to remember that if I allow anything, even something good, to take Your place in my heart, I'll miss what is best.

You are the pearl of lasting value. At the end of my life, so many of these other things will fade in significance. Help me to live today with eternity in mind. Help me to prioritize so that I truly put You first in thought and in action. Help me to trust You when the other things I want don't fall into place. May I remember that You promise to provide whatever I need—not whatever I want. I need to be filled by You. Help me to clear room in my heart so that I can create a home for You there. Come dwell within me. Light a fire in the hearth of my soul. Come, Holy Spirit.

Day Two
THE PROBLEM OF THE HEART

Read Jeremiah 17:9 (NAB)

1. When Jeremiah implored his people to obey God, he understood that the heart of the problem was the problem of the heart. How did he describe the heart in Jeremiah 17:9?

2. A. In what way did the state of the human heart make it difficult for the Israelites to keep the covenant—to follow the Ten Commandments?

    B. If it was going to be so hard for the Israelites to keep the law, why was the law given? See CCC 62.

The law served the purpose of showing the Israelites how desperately they needed a Savior. They couldn't keep the law. They needed help. God was forming His people to recognize their helplessness, yet He never wanted them to feel hopeless. **Helpless, but not hopeless.** One of the reasons that God continually pointed the Israelites to a coming Savior (and think of how many examples of this we've seen in our study this year!) was to instill in them a hope of something (someone) better yet to come.

3. The state of the heart wasn't just an Old Testament concern. What do we learn from Luke 6:45?

4. How is the heart described in CCC 2563?

So often, we mistakenly think that the problem is our external behaviors, when it's actually the state of our hearts. The heart is where we make decisions—it's the home of our passions, our will, and our motivations. Our priorities come from our hearts. Our words and actions flow out of what is in our hearts. The heart as God originally created it was good. Its inclination was to do good. But once sin entered the world, our hearts became "crooked." Left on their own, they are naturally inclined to lead us toward whatever feels good in the moment rather than what is morally right and best.

5. Discuss how an unwillingness to recognize the "crookedness" of the heart is an enormous block to experiencing conversion of heart. (For an explanation of what is meant by "conversion of heart," see Appendix 5, Conversion of Heart)

Quiet your heart and enjoy His presence. . . . He wants to hear what's on your heart.

The starting point for all of us is recognizing that we have a need. It's to admit that on our own, we aren't doing so well. Do any of the following thoughts ring true for you?

"I'm afraid of not being liked."
"I hate to look in the mirror. I'm just reminded of the weight I need to lose."
"I sometimes wonder if this is all that there is. This is what life is supposed to be about?"
"I'm so sick of falling into the same bad habits, time and time again. I never seem to progress."
"I'm afraid of getting cancer. I'm afraid to die."
"I wonder if my teenagers love me. I've given them all I've got, but the way they treat me makes me feel worthless."
"I'm afraid that my husband will leave me."
"I feel like I can't both be a good mom and do all I need to do at work."

We all have fears. We all have needs. We can cover them up by pretending that they aren't there. We can get busy to distract ourselves. We can do whatever it takes to be liked, even if it means compromise. We can slap on a happy face and try to convince ourselves that it isn't so bad. We can turn to alcohol to take off the edge. But the underlying issues will remain and rob us of sleep and peace.

Jesus cares deeply about all these things that are going on within our hearts. He came to point us to a better way. His way doesn't cover things up—it exposes them to the warmth of His merciful love. Take some time in His soothing presence to tell Him all the ways in which you need Him.

Day Three
THE SOLUTION TO THE PROBLEM OF THE HEART

Read Jeremiah 31:33–36 and 33:14–17.

To understand this passage, it's important to remember what God's purpose was when He made covenants with His people in the Old Testament. While a contract is a business agreement in which one party gives something and the other gives something in return, a covenant is a sharing of persons. It's a gift of self. Throughout the Bible, we read of many covenants that God made with the Israelites. In each one, His purpose was the same. He was drawing them into a relationship with Him. He was creating a family.

God wanted to create a family that would serve as a beacon of hope to the surrounding nations, shouting of the difference that it makes to have the LORD as your God. But the hearts of the Israelites kept getting in the way. Instead of choosing things that would draw them closer to God, they made choices that distanced themselves from Him.

When Jeremiah spoke of a New Covenant, its purpose and the purpose of the Old Covenant were one and the same. God wanted (and wants) to draw people into a relationship with Him as a loving Father.

1. How did Jeremiah describe the New Covenant in Jeremiah 31:33–34?

2. How does Jeremiah 33:14–17 point to the fulfillment of God's covenant with David?

3. The New Covenant would come about because the terms of the Old Covenant would be satisfied. Justice would be served. How would this occur? See CCC 580.

Our Father keeps His promises. He kept His promise to David, He kept His promise to the Israelites, and He'll keep His promise to you and me. He is a keeper of the covenant, and when we have proved incapable or unwilling to keep up our side of the bargain, He has stepped in and paid the price for our failing.

4. Justice was served when Jesus paid the price for our sin. Because He died in our place, we can become something that we weren't before. Who can we become, and how is that consistent with God's steady purpose in both the Old and the New Covenants? See 1 John 3:1.

5. The New Covenant was to have the same purpose as the Old Covenant—bringing people into the family of God—but there would be radical differences. The New Covenant would come with power. It would be written on the heart, and have the power to *change* that heart. What is the source of that power? See Acts 1:8.

Quiet your heart and enjoy His presence. . . . Transformation happens as we pray.

Because of Jesus, you have a new heart and a new identity. As it says in 2 Corinthians 5:17, "Therefore, if any one is in Christ, he is a new creation; the old has passed away, behold, the new has come!" You are now the adopted daughter of your Father. How does He see you? He sees you as His precious daughter. Nothing more, nothing less. You might say, "But I don't feel it!" But that is who you are. We don't achieve this through effort. It isn't something that we have to obtain. The work is in recognition and awareness. We need to recognize what is already there. You are God's beloved daughter. You already have this dignity. You just need to begin to let go of your blindness, the faulty way you see yourself, and start acting like God's beloved daughter.

The starting point for this change is prayer. As you pray, the Holy Spirit is released to transform you from the inside out. Your heavenly Father loves you too much to leave you as you are. God wants to mold you into a woman who serves as a beacon of hope to a broken world. Our world is desperate to see something that works. People want to see a faith that makes a difference. A friend's example and testimony carries far more weight than historical authority and tradition. People are asking, "Does it work?" and then are looking at us to find the answer. They are observing.

Oh Lord! Please, may our hearts not get in the way! Help us to choose the things that will draw us closer to You, and may we literally run from the choices that distance us from You.

Day Four
HOW WILL HE GIVE US A NEW HEART?

Read Ezekiel 36:25–27.

1. A. What is the first thing that God promised to do in this passage? See Ezekiel 36:26.

B. According to CCC 1432, why do we need a new heart? What's wrong with the old one? What should be our response to this gift of a new heart?

What happens when we don't confess our sins? Our hearts grow hard and callused. We become less sensitive to God, and prone to further sin. To keep our hearts soft, we should take advantage of the wonderful gift of reconciliation. In addition to that, we should confess sin daily. Why would we let a moment go by with unconfessed sin hardening our hearts?

2. What does God's Spirit do in the new heart of a woman? See Ezekiel 36:27.

3. What does CCC 694 say that water symbolizes?

4. We first receive the gift of the Holy Spirit in baptism. This is when we become "a new creation" (2 Corinthians 5:17). We are sealed with the Holy Spirit in confirmation (CCC 1304). Yet many of us, although we've received the sacraments of baptism and confirmation, aren't experiencing the power of the Holy Spirit in our personal lives. We hear people talk about the strength they receive from the Holy Spirit, the breaking of sinful habits, and the peace that passes understanding, and we wonder why we aren't experiencing the same thing. We might wonder, "Did I just get skipped when the Holy Spirit was passed out?" The answer is no. But for many of us, what we received in baptism and confirmation is like a credit card that hasn't been activated. If you have received a new credit card but haven't made the phone call to activate it, you aren't able to use it. In that same way, we need to activate the gifts we've received in the sacraments by experiencing conversion of heart. See Appendix 5 for a more in-depth explanation of this. Take

some time to think about your faith journey. Are you experiencing the difference that the indwelling Holy Spirit makes? Record any insights below.

Quiet your heart and enjoy His presence. . . . You are the glove; He is the hand.

What would you give to be able to go to Jesus directly with your problems? How would you like to hear one of His parables from His own mouth? What difference would it make to look into Jesus' eyes of love and hear Him say, "You did not choose me, but I chose you" (John 15:16)?

This was the experience of the disciples. So imagine how shocking it was for them to hear Jesus' words in John 16:7, "I tell you the truth, it is better for you that I go. For if I do not go, the Advocate will not come to you. But if I go, I will send him to you." It's better if He goes? It must have seemed unbelievable to them. What could be better than having Jesus, in the flesh, at their fingertips?

Little did they know that when Jesus ascended to heaven, the Advocate (the Holy Spirit) was going to come to live in them, giving them new hearts. These hearts would be so utterly transformed that they would go on to change the world. The Holy Spirit made the seemingly impossible possible.

What is it in your life that requires strength beyond your own? Are you facing something for which an evaluation of your resources reveals that you don't have what it takes? Be assured, the indwelling Holy Spirit makes all the difference.

"The sight of seemingly impossible tasks . . . are not sent to discourage us. They come to motivate us to attempt spiritual feats that would be impossible except for the great strength God has placed within us through His indwelling Holy Spirit. Difficulties are sent in order to reveal what God can do in answer to faith that prays and works."[21]

---

[21] Ibid., 73.

Day Five
HOW POWERFUL IS GOD'S SPIRIT?

Read Ezekiel 37:1–14.

1. In order to illustrate the power of God's Spirit, God gave Ezekiel a vision of a graveyard with dry bones. The utter dryness of the bones emphasized the fact that they had been there a long time and were completely devoid of life. God asked Ezekiel to prophesy over them that they were to come to life. What would make that miracle possible? See Ezekiel 37:5.

2. Describe what the bones and God's action in them represented. See Ezekiel 37:11–14.

3. What made all the difference to the dry bones? Breath! With breath comes life. Without it, we die. Psalm 39:6 (NAB) reminds us that each person's life is but a breath. It's fragile. *We're* fragile. A visit to the intensive care unit of a hospital, a funeral, or a child with an asthma attack brings this truth home. The Hebrew word translated "breath" is *ru-ah*, which is also translated "spirit." Over and over again in the Old Testament, this same word is used to describe *God's* Spirit.[22] Therein lies the paradox: On the one hand, we are fragile. We depend on God for every breath. Yet at the same time, we've been breathed into by God Himself, the Creator of the universe. He breathes His Holy Spirit into us. Discuss what difference that makes in our daily lives based on 2 Timothy 1:7.

---

[22] Numbers 24:2; Judges 3:10, 11:29, 13:25, 14:19, 15:14; 1 Samuel 10:6, 10:10, 11:6, 16:13, 19:20, 19:23; 2 Samuel 23:2; 2 Chronicles 15:1, 18:23, 20:14; Job 33:4; Isaiah 11:2, 32:15, 61:1, 63:10–11, 63:14; Ezekiel 2:2, 3:12, 8:3, 11:1, 11:5.

4. What Ezekiel saw was powerful and encouraging, but in that moment it was a vision, not reality. When did God truly bring life from death? See Acts 2:24.

Quiet your heart and enjoy His presence. . . . His Holy Spirit makes the impossible possible.

"Having the eyes of your hearts enlightened, that you may know . . . what is the immeasurable greatness of his power in us who believe, according to the working of his great might which he accomplished in Christ when he raised him from the dead and made him sit at his right hand in the heavenly places . . ." (Ephesians 1:18–20).

The same Spirit that was powerful enough to raise Jesus from the dead is available to us. No matter how hopeless our situation is—no matter how much it feels as dead as dry bones—God's resurrection power can breathe new restorative life into it. Yes, we are fragile, but because Christ's Holy Spirit dwells within us, we can scale mountains! Jesus said, "Truly, I say to you, if you have faith and never doubt . . . if you say to this mountain, 'Be taken up and cast into the sea,' it will be done. And whatever you ask in prayer, you will receive, if you have faith" (Matthew 21:21–22). Ask God to pour out His Spirit on you. Ask Him to release all the gifts of the Spirit that you need. He is just waiting to shower you with wisdom, strength, and spiritual healing. "If you . . . know how to give good gifts to your children, how much more will your Father in heaven give good things to those who ask him!" (Matthew 7:11)

Conclusion

As the exiled Israelite people listened to the words of Jeremiah and Ezekiel, they received hope that one day God would restore them and bring them home. They knew they had broken the covenant, but they looked forward to a day when the New Covenant would come.

The longing to return home was satisfied after seventy years of exile in Babylon. The world power at that time was Persia, and it was ruled by King Cyrus. Cyrus had been mentioned by name approximately 150 years before by the prophet Isaiah:

> Thus says the LORD, your Redeemer . . . who confirms the words of my servant, and performs the counsel of his messengers; who says to Jerusalem, "She shall be inhabited," and of the cities of Judah, "They shall be built, and I will raise up their ruins" . . . who says of Cyrus, "He is my shepherd, and he

shall fulfil all my purpose"; saying of Jerusalem, "She shall be built," and of the temple, "Your foundation shall be laid." Thus says the LORD to his anointed, Cyrus, whose right hand I have grasped, to subdue nations before him, and uncover the loins of kings, to open doors before him, that gates may not be closed . . . For the sake of my servant Jacob, and Israel my chosen, I call you by your name, I surnamed you, though you do not know me … I have aroused him righteousness, and I will make straight all his ways; he shall build my city and set my exiles free. (Isaiah 44:24, 26, 28; Isaiah 45:1, 4, 13)

At a time when Persia wasn't a world power and Isaiah couldn't have possibly known who Cyrus was, God told Isaiah that this specific person would be His chosen instrument to bring the people back to the Promised Land. King Cyrus wasn't a Jew. He didn't even know God. But God chose to subdue nations before him for the sake of Israel. God wasn't limited by Cyrus' disbelief in Him; He can choose to use anyone in order to bring about His purposes.

King Cyrus allowed the Jews to return, and the Persians helped them with gifts of silver, gold, and precious items so that they could rebuild the temple. Just as the people had been deported to Babylon in three stages, they were allowed to return in three stages. The temple eventually was rebuilt, but it never returned to the glory of the days of Solomon's rule. The Israelites were back in the Promised Land, but they were ruled by the Persians, then the Greeks, and finally the Romans. The people longed not just to be home, but to be free.

True freedom would come, but it wouldn't be political freedom. As the people waited to see what the New Covenant would bring, God sent the prophet Malachi to continue to give them hope. Malachi said that before the day of the Lord would come, a messenger would appear who would prepare the way: "Behold, I will send you Eli´jah the prophet before the great and awesome day of the LORD comes. And he will turn the hearts of fathers to their children and the hearts of children to their fathers" (Malachi 4:5–6). So the Jews waited in expectation. They were on the lookout for a messenger who would prepare the way for their rescuer.

This messenger was John the Baptist, and he prepared the way for the One who would come to rescue us all. The homecoming and release from captivity that the Israelites longed for resonates with us and our desire for safety, belonging, and freedom. The Israelites weren't the only ones to break the covenant. We have failed to obey God as well. God looks at all of His children with love and says, "I've prepared a new way for you to come home. Whatever you've done, whatever you've become, you can have a fresh start. Let me give you a new heart. Ask me to take your heart of stone and replace it with a heart of flesh." God's Spirit can breathe new life into dead bones. It can empower you to live as you want to live. This life of power and victory is yours for the asking. Come home to the banquet God has prepared for you.

My Resolution

In what specific way will I apply what I learned in this lesson?

Examples:

1. I'm done running from God. I'm tired of covering up my sin. I'm going to go to reconciliation this week and lay it all before Him, holding nothing back. I'll let the fire of His love and mercy burn away my sin.

2. If I'm honest, I have to admit that I can always find time to do what matters most to me. This week, I'll put God first, and instead of rushing my lesson preparation at the end of the week, I'll make time every day for prayer and Bible study.

3. Instead of starting my day with my to-do list, the very first thing I'll do is pray. I'll roll out of my bed onto my knees, and give God my day. I'll ask Him to help me to avoid going after emptiness. I'll ask for the Holy Spirit to fill me with everything I need for the day ahead. Instead of relying on my own strength, I'll rely on His.

My resolution:

Catechism Clips

CCC 62 After the patriarchs, God formed Israel as his people by freeing them from slavery in Egypt. He established with them the covenant of Mount Sinai and, through Moses, gave them his law so that they would recognize him and serve him as the one living and true God, the provident Father and just judge, and so that they would look for the promised Savior.

CCC 580 The perfect fulfillment of the Law could be the work of none but the divine legislator, born subject to the Law in the person of the Son. In Jesus, the Law no longer appears engraved on tables of stone but "upon the heart" of the Servant who becomes "a covenant to the people," because he will "faithfully bring forth justice." Jesus fulfills the Law to the point of taking upon himself "the curse of the Law" incurred by those who do not "abide by the things written in the book of the Law, and do them," for his death took place to redeem them "from the transgressions under the first covenant."

Symbol of the Holy Spirit

CCC 694 *Water.* The symbolism of water signifies the Holy Spirit's action in Baptism, since after the invocation of the Holy Spirit it becomes the efficacious sacramental sign of new birth: just as the gestation of our first birth took place in water, so the water of Baptism truly signifies that our birth into the divine life is given to us in the Holy Spirit. As "by one Spirit we were all baptized," so we are also "made to drink of one Spirit." Thus the Spirit is also personally the living water welling up from Christ crucified as its source and welling up in us to eternal life.

CCC 1432 The human heart is heavy and hardened. God must give man a new heart. Conversion is first of all a work of the grace of God who makes our hearts return to him: "Restore us to thyself, O LORD, that we may be restored!" God gives us the strength to begin anew. It is in discovering the greatness of God's love that our heart is shaken by the horror and weight of sin and begins to fear offending God by sin and being separated from him. The human heart is converted by looking upon him whom our sins have pierced:

> Let us fix our eyes on Christ's blood and understand how precious it is to his Father, for, poured out for our salvation it has brought to the whole world the grace of repentance.

CCC 2563 The heart is the dwelling-place where I am, where I live; according to the Semitic or Biblical expression, the heart is the place "to which I withdraw." The heart is our hidden center, beyond the grasp of our reason and of others; only the Spirit of God can fathom the human heart and know it fully. The heart is the place of decision, deeper than our psychic drives. It is the place of truth, where we choose life or death. It is the place of encounter, because as image of God we live in relation: it is the place of covenant.

Verse Study

See Appendix 3 for instructions on how to complete a verse study.

1 Thessalonians 5:19

1. Verse:

2. Paraphrase:

3. Questions:

4. Cross-references:

5. Personal Application:

Lesson 8

THE THRONE ROOM

Introduction

The story is told of a student of Saint Bonaventure who asked him, "Why do men not love God?" Saint Bonaventure answered, "They don't love him because they don't know him." I pray that as you've studied Christ in the Old Testament, you have grown in knowledge of who Jesus is. Even more than that, I pray that your love for Him has grown because you know Him better.

The story of **Creation** teaches us that Jesus created the world (Colossians 1:16) and now offers us the chance to have a fresh start, to become "new creations" (2 Corinthians 5:17).

The story of **the Fall** teaches us that Jesus was alienated so that we could regain the intimacy lost by Adam and Eve.

The story of **Noah** teaches us that Jesus is our ark of safety and refuge. We can hide in Him.

The story of the **Tower of Babel** teaches us that Christ, not the greatness of our own names, is the true source of our significance.

The story of **Abraham** teaches us that all the promises of God are yes in Jesus (2 Corinthians 1:20).

The story of **Joseph** and the famine teaches us that Jesus, the bread from heaven, satisfies our hunger.

The story of **Moses** teaches us that Jesus is our deliverer.

The story of **Joshua** teaches us that Jesus broke down the walls that prevented us from drawing close to God.

The story of **David** teaches us that Jesus was the promised Son of David who would sit on an eternal throne, and He was worth the wait.

The passages in the **Psalms** teaches us that we can approach Jesus honestly with all our emotions and that He completely understands and empathizes because He, too, has experienced human difficulty.

The story of **the Temple** teaches us that Jesus' atoning sacrifice made it possible for us to draw near to God.

The story of **Isaiah** teaches us that Jesus' death on the cross wasn't God's plan gone awry. It was exactly when the battle was won.

The story of **Jeremiah and Ezekiel** teaches us that Jesus will give us new hearts that are filled with the power of the Holy Spirit.

One of the wonderful things about Jesus is that He is so magnificent, so indescribable, so praiseworthy that we will never finish getting to know Him while we walk this earth. There will always be more to discover. This is the relationship of a lifetime, and the more we know Him, the more we'll love Him.

This week's lesson gives us a glimpse of what it will be like to behold Christ's glory in heaven. As we open the Bible, the curtain will be pulled back and we will look at Saint John's vision of the throne room of God.

Day One
JESUS IS WORTHY

Read Revelation 5:1–6.

Helpful Info:

The one who sits on the throne is God.
The scroll is a papyrus roll possibly containing a list of afflictions for sinners (see Ezekiel 2:9–10) or God's plan for the world (symbolized by the number 7).
The seven seals indicate the importance of the message, totally hidden from all but God.[23]

---

[23] Life Teen, ed., Revelation 5:1 footnote in the *New American Bible* (Phoenix: Life Teen, 2009), 384.

The Throne Room | 8

1. A mighty angel asked the question, "Who is worthy to open the scroll and break its seals?" In this context, the word *worthy* means "drawing down a scale to assign the matching value." What was the answer given in verse 3 to the angel's question? How is this truth confirmed in Ecclesiastes 7:20?

2. How is the One who can solve this dilemma described? See Revelation 5:5, Genesis 49:9, Isaiah 11:1, and Revelation 22:16.

3. Why was the lion of Judah allowed to open the scroll? See Revelation 5:4.

4. A. Based on verse 5, what animal would you expect to see coming to open the scroll in verse 6? What animal came instead?

    B. Why is Jesus called the Lamb of God? See Genesis 22:8 and Exodus 12:1–8.

5. The Lamb had seven horns and seven eyes. These are identified as the seven spirits of God that were sent into the world. Seven is the biblical number representing wholeness or completeness.[24] The horns denote power, and the eyes, knowledge. In what way does the Holy Spirit bring power and knowledge to our lives? See Acts 1:8 and CCC 1831.

---

[24] Life Teen, ed., Revelation 1:4 footnote in the *New American Bible*, 379.

Quiet your heart and enjoy His presence. . . . The Lamb has triumphed.

In this vision, Jesus appeared as a slaughtered lamb. The wounds were not evidence of defeat, but evidence of His victory. All of mankind was in desperate straits—truly in a hopeless situation. The wages of sin was eternal death, and there was no person on earth without sin. How would we ever regain what had been lost? Thank God that He sent a Savior to do for us what we couldn't do for ourselves.

Jesus came to fight and to rescue us. This is what He was doing on the cross. He was going to war against all the demonic forces, against the powers and dominions we can't fight against. He was invading enemy territory- the world that the enemy thought was under His control- and Jesus took it back.

It was the invasion of one kingdom by a stronger kingdom. The invasion of the kingdom of death and sin and hell by another kingdom- a stronger kingdom- the kingdom of God. The invasion of the kingdom of darkness by God's Kingdom of light. What looked like defeat- crucifixion- the most degrading, humiliating, stripping, agonizing death imaginable- was actually Jesus going to war for you and me.

When Jesus died for our sins and then rose again, Satan was disarmed and defeated. He was stripped of his destructive weapon- death. He was also stripped of his favorite weapon as the accuser- the ability to accuse us before God that we are guilty. When Jesus died in our place, God said that now nothing can separate us from the love of God. The price for our sin has been paid. The Lamb has triumphed.

Day Two
JESUS PURCHASED US FOR GOD

Read Revelation 5:8–10.

1. A. What was the fitting response of the four living creatures and the twenty-four elders[25] to the worthiness of the Lamb?

---

[25] The "twenty-four 'elders'" (in Greek, *presbyteroi*, whence the English 'priest') replicate the twenty-four priestly divisions who served in the Temple in any given year." Scott Hahn, *The Lamb's Supper* (New York: Doubleday, 1999), 68.

B. This vision should give us a fresh perspective on what we're asking for in the Our Father when we pray, "Thy will be done on earth as it is in heaven." How is God's will done in heaven? God's will is done by all responding to Jesus with worship. If we truly mean what we pray in the Our Father, then we will follow the examples of the creatures and elders in heaven by responding to Jesus with worship. What does "falling down before the Lamb" look like in your life?

2. Each of the elders held a bowl filled with incense. This incense was the prayers of the holy ones, the saints. What does this have to do with us? See Psalm 141:2.

3. In what sense is Revelation 5:9 a vision of the restoration of what was lost at the Tower of Babel?

4. After Jesus purchased people with His blood, what did He make them?

While the Israelites had prided themselves on being the chosen nation, selected by God from all the people on the earth, Revelation 5:10 is a picture of inclusion. It's a reflection of Christ's desire to "make disciples of *all* nations" (Matthew 28:19). The bride of Christ (the Church) is all the more beautiful because of its diversity.

5. A. In 1 Peter 2:4–5, we are encouraged to "come to [Jesus], to that living stone, rejected by men but in God's sight chosen and precious; and like living stones be yourselves built into a spiritual house, to be a holy priesthood, to offer spiritual sacrifices acceptable to God through Jesus Christ." According to CCC 901, what are the spiritual sacrifices we can offer as laywomen?

B. We are made sharers in the priestly office of Christ through our baptism (CCC 897). In this role, we are to bring Christ to others. What can we learn from 2 Corinthians 2:14 about how we are to do this?

Quiet your heart and enjoy His presence. . . . Jesus purchased you for God.

"You were bought with a price" (1 Corinthians 6:20).

"You know that you were ransomed from the futile ways inherited from your fathers, not with perishable things such as silver or gold, but with the precious blood of Christ, like that of a lamb without blemish or spot" (1 Peter 1:18–19).

A slave was considered ransomed when someone paid money to purchase that slave's freedom. Without Jesus, we are slaves to sin. We're slaves to the worst parts of ourselves, utterly lacking the ability to experience inner transformation. We may mistakenly think that doing whatever we feel like is freedom, but the truth is, it's the worst kind of slavery. When Jesus ransomed us through His blood—something far more precious than writing a check—He purchased our freedom. Now we are "set free from sin, [and] have become slaves of righteousness" (Romans 6:18).

> *In certain skilled crafts, an apprentice works under a master, who trains, shapes, and molds his apprentice in the finer points of his craft. All people choose a master and pattern themselves after him. Without Jesus, we would have no choice—we would have to apprentice ourselves to sin, and the results would be guilt, suffering, and separation from God. Thanks to Jesus, however, we can now choose God as our Master. Following him, we can enjoy new life and learn how to work for him. Are you still serving your first master, sin? Or have you apprenticed yourself to God?*[26]

Day Three
JESUS IS THE LORD OF HOSTS

Read Revelation 5:11–14.

---

[26] Life Application, ed., Romans 6:16–18 footnote in the New International Version Bible (Wheaton, IL: Tyndale House, 1991), 2038.

The Throne Room | 8

1. How many angels surrounded the Lamb on the throne? What were they doing?

2. One of Jesus' titles is the Lord of Hosts. This multitude, or host, of angels is an army ready to do His bidding on earth and in heaven. This mobilized host of angels is seen throughout Scripture.[27] The title Lord of Hosts is also used many times in the Bible. In what context is it used in Isaiah 6:1–2? At what point during Mass do we say this particular name of the Lord?

3. What seven things did the angels ascribe to Jesus in their hymn of praise in Revelation 5:12?

4. Revelation 4 records the vision of the throne of God, prior to the appearance of the Lamb of God. "Behold, a throne stood in heaven, with one seated on the throne! And he who sat on there appeared like jasper and carnelian, and round the throne was a rainbow that looked like an emerald" (Revelation 4:2–3). Twenty-four elders worshipped Him saying, "Worthy are you, our Lord and God, to receive glory and honor and power, for you created all things, and by your will they existed and were created" (Revelation 4:11). The same words are used to describe the One seated on the throne and the Lamb. What additional insight into the unity and equality of God the Father and God the Son is found in CCC 449?

5. The worship of the Lamb of God crescendos when "every creature in heaven and on earth and under the earth and in the sea, and all therein, saying, 'To him who sits upon the throne and to the Lamb be blessing and honor and glory and might

---

[27] "The Lord came from Sinai ... he came from the ten thousands of holy ones" (Deuteronomy 33:2); "Is there any number to his armies? Upon whom does his light not arise?" (Job 25:3); "Thrones were placed and one that was ancient of days took his seat ... a thousand thousands served him, and ten thousand times ten thousand stood before him" (Daniel 7:9–10).

for ever and ever'" (Revelation 5:13). According to Philippians 2:10–11, what should be our response to the Lamb of God?

Quiet your heart and enjoy His presence. . . . Jesus is the Lord of Hosts.

"The Lord is my light and my salvation; whom shall I fear? The Lord is the stronghold of my life; of whom shall I fear?" (Psalm 27:1)

Whenever we face a circumstance that seems daunting, overwhelming, or even frightening, we can be strengthened by meditating on Jesus, the Lord of Hosts. He goes before us, stands behind us and is always at our side. There is no one stronger, no one more faithful, no one more valiant, no one more in control. He commands angel armies who fight on our behalf.

Think about that: We are surrounded on all sides by God, who can command legions of angels to come to our aid. He reigns forever on earth and in heaven, yet offers us personal friendship. No matter how much darkness surrounds us on the battlefield of life, Christ is our light.

In the words of Peter Kreeft, "The devil is not like a dragon but like Dracula: he flees from the light. He is actually afraid of you insofar as you have Christ in your soul. The devil is also afraid of your guardian angel, who is a 'being of light'. Darkness fears light. Pray to the angel God has appointed to guard you when you are tempted. Only important people in the world get bodyguards, but each of us is so important to God that He has given each of us a Heavenly soul-guard."[28]

Day Four
JESUS IS MAKING ALL THINGS NEW

Read Revelation 21:3–7.

The Helpful Info on Day One says, "The one who sits on the throne is God." Because Jesus is God, we are free to apply all descriptions of God on the throne in Revelation 21 to Christ.

---

[28] Peter Kreeft, *Practical Theology* (San Francisco, CA: Ignatius Press, 2014), 124.

The Throne Room | 8

1. In Revelation 21:3, God promises to eternally dwell with His people. This has been His desire from the very beginning. Describe God's progression of intimacy throughout Scripture.

   Note: The phrase "the dwelling of God" comes from the Greek word *skenen*, which means "tent, tabernacle."

   A. What was the level of intimacy in the Garden of Eden before Adam and Eve sinned?

   B. What did God command that Moses and the Israelites construct so that He could be closer to them?

   C. What did Solomon build, and how did this bring the Israelites closer to God?

   D. What major progression in intimacy is described in John 1:14?

   E. How did God's intimacy with His children grow at Pentecost? This is what Jesus promised in John 14:23.

   F. As Catholics, what special intimacy are we allowed to experience with God? See Mark 14:22–26.

   G. When God dwells with us, face-to-face, in heaven, how long will it last?

2. What will be some of the benefits of God dwelling with us in heaven? See Revelation 21:4.

3. "And he who sat upon the throne said, 'Behold, I make all things new'" (Revelation 21:5). In which area of your life do you need to experience renewal? What do you want God to "make new" in your life?

4. "I am the Alpha and the Omega, the beginning and the end" (Revelation 21:6). Read the following chart, "The Beginning and the End."[29] Jesus, the Alpha and Omega, was there at the beginning. He was there when mankind fell and sin entered the world. The events described in Genesis set the stage for our universal need for rescue. Jesus will also be there at the end, when our victorious rescue, described in Revelation, will be complete. This chart describes the fall at the beginning (Genesis) and the victory won by Christ that we'll experience in heaven (Revelation). Choose one of the following victories and record what it means to you personally.

Genesis	*Revelation*
The sun is created	The sun is not needed
Satan is victorious	Satan is defeated
Sin enters the human race	Sin is banished
People run and hide from God	People are invited to live with God forever
People are cursed	The curse is removed
Tears are shed, with sorrow for sin	No more sin, no more tears or sorrow
The garden and the earth are cursed	God's city is glorified, the earth is made new
The fruit from the tree of life is not to be eaten	God's people may eat from the tree of life
Paradise is lost	Paradise is regained
People are doomed to death	Death is defeated, believers live forever with God

---

[29] Life Application, ed., study note from Revelation in the New International Version Bible, 2331.

5. The life-giving water spoken of in Revelation 21:6 was also offered by Jesus to the Samaritan woman in John 4:14. What is this water? What does it represent?

Quiet your heart and enjoy His presence. . . . Your King is victorious.

"[She] who conquers shall have this heritage, and I will be [her] God, and [she] shall be my [daughter]" (Revelation 21:7).

You are a victorious daughter, and your Father is the King of kings. You belong to Him. His love for you flows from the depths of eternity. There is nothing you face alone. Your Father stands behind you. He infuses you with strength so that you can bear and overcome all that you face, achieving victories in the spiritual life you never imagined possible.

"It is the Spirit himself bearing witness with our spirit that we are children of God, and if children, then heirs, heirs of God and fellow heirs with Christ" (Romans 8:16). The Holy Spirit assures us that we belong to God, and that He is going to shower us with a heavenly inheritance. There are also gifts we receive on earth. One of the most beautiful of those gifts is "God's love [being] poured into our hearts through the Holy Spirit who has been given to us" (Romans 5:5).

Spend a few minutes meditating on what it means to be a victorious daughter of the King of kings.

Day Five
SEEING HIM FACE-TO-FACE

1. Saint Paul offered a glimpse of the day when we will behold Christ's glory. Read 1 Corinthians 13:12, noting what it will be like when we see Him face-to-face.

2. How is heaven described in 1 Corinthians 2:9 and CCC 1027?

3. When we see Jesus in heaven, we will receive rewards for how we have lived. What do the following verses teach about our heavenly reward?

   Matthew 16:27

   1 Corinthians 3:12–14

4. What honor will be given in heaven to those who persevere on earth?

During our time on earth, there will be many things we have to endure. Often, we'll have to "die to self" in order to be faithful to God. Each one of those sacrifices—each one of those times when we could have had a selfish response but instead chose to persevere—will be rewarded. If we endure and persevere, we will *reign* with Christ in heaven.

5. James 1:12 and Revelation 2:10 describe something that will be given to those who endure and remain faithful to God. What is it?

Quiet your heart and enjoy His presence. . . . He is preparing a place for you.

You're going to receive a beautiful crown in heaven. When this happens, all that you are experiencing right now for His *sake, every bit of it, will feel worth that priceless crown. What will you do with that crown when you receive it? Perhaps you'll respond the same way the twenty-four elders did in Revelation 4:10–11, because of your wholehearted love for the Lord:*

> . . . *the twenty-four elders fall down before him who is seated on the throne and worship him who lives for ever and ever; they cast their crowns before the throne, singing:*

"Worthy are you, our Lord and God,
to receive glory and honor and power,
for you created all things,
and by your will they existed and were created."

He is worthy.
He is worth it.

Persevere, precious daughter of God. In this world, you will have trouble. There will be more expected of you than you feel able to handle. There will be times of pain and pressure. But never forget, the everlasting arms are underneath you.

"*The eternal God is your dwelling place, and underneath are the everlasting arms. And he thrust out the enemy before you*" (Deuteronomy 33:27).

Conclusion

We all want to be happy. This is something all people have in common, along with not wanting to be lied to or deceived. These deep desires will drive us to choose certain friends, specific pursuits, and will impact how we order our priorities.

Many of us have believed that if we just had wealth, we'd be happy. Some of us wise up to the fact that contentment will always be illusive if we pin our hopes on wealth, because we always want just a little bit more. "For what does it profit a man, to gain the whole world and forfeit his life?" (Mark 8:36)

Many believe that being honored, being admired is the key to happiness. But honor and admiration reside in the mind and heart of the person doing the honoring and doing the admiring. Happiness is something that we want inside of *us*. All the accolades in the world don't fill up what is empty within.

So what about power? Will that bring us ultimate happiness? No again. Power is something we can use to pursue good, but it is a means, not an end. Is health the game changer? If I have good health, do I have it all? Philosopher Peter Kreeft would argue that the body is important, but that "you do not 'have' a soul in the same sense that you 'have' a body; you *are* a soul (emphasis mine)."[30]

---

[30] Peter Kreeft, *Practical Theology* (San Francisco, CA: Ignatius Press, 2014), 164.

Nothing will ultimately satisfy us and make us happy like God. This is why heaven is going to be so amazing. We'll want nothing but Him, and He will be enough. Just looking at Him, experiencing the beatific vision, will fill us with a sense of total fulfillment, and zero boredom. There will always be something new to learn about God- some new facet to discover. God alone can fill us. But He is a gentleman and will never force Himself on us. It's up to us to daily open up our hearts to Him and invite Him in.

1 Corinthians 13:12 tells us that, "Now we see in a mirror dimly, but then face to face. Now I know in part; then I shall understand fully, even as I have been fully understood." This is what heaven will feel like- all confusion gone, all doubts swept away, being fully known and understood, and being utterly fascinated by what lies before us. This is what God is preparing for us.

My Resolution

In what specific way will I apply what I learned in this lesson?

Examples:

1. I will pray the Litany of Praise (Appendix 6) throughout the summer to remind myself of who Jesus is and all He longs to do for me.

2. I will make a list of all the benefits and gifts I receive because I am a victorious daughter of the King of kings.

3. I'll read Revelation 4 and 5 before the Blessed Sacrament, meditating on heaven.

My resolution:

Catechism Clips

CCC 449 By attributing to Jesus the divine title "Lord," the first confessions of the Church's faith affirm from the beginning that the power, honor and glory due to God the Father are due also to Jesus, because "he was in the form of God," and the Father manifested the sovereignty of Jesus by raising him from the dead and exalting him into his glory.

CCC 901 "Hence the laity, dedicated as they are to Christ and anointed by the Holy Spirit, are marvelously called and prepared so that even richer fruits of the Spirit may be produced in them. For all their works, prayers, and apostolic undertakings, family and married life, daily work, relaxation of mind and body, if they are accomplished in the Spirit—indeed even the hardships of life if patiently born—all these become spiritual sacrifices acceptable to God through Jesus Christ. In the celebration of the Eucharist these may most fittingly be offered to the Father along with the body of the Lord. And so, worshipping everywhere by their holy actions, the laity consecrate the world itself to God, everywhere offering worship by the holiness of their lives."

CCC 1027 This mystery of blessed communion with God and all who are in Christ is beyond all understanding and description. Scripture speaks of it in images: life, light, peace, wedding feast, wine of the kingdom, the Father's house, the heavenly Jerusalem, paradise: "no eye has seen, nor ear heard, nor the heart of man conceived, what God has prepared for those who love him."

CCC 1831 The seven *gifts* of the Holy Spirit are wisdom, understanding, counsel, fortitude, knowledge, piety, and fear of the Lord. They belong in their fullness to Christ, Son of David. They complete and perfect the virtues of those who receive them. They make the faithful docile in readily obeying divine inspirations.

Verse Study

See Appendix 3 for instructions on how to complete a verse study.

Revelation 22:17.

1. Verse:

2. Paraphrase:

3. Questions:

4. Cross-references:

5. Personal Application:

Lesson 9: Connect Coffee Talk
JESUS – I'M DESERVING OF WORSHIP

Accompanying talk can be viewed by DVD or digital download purchase or access online at walkingwithpurpose.com/videos.

"In the year King Uzziah died, I saw the Lord seated on a high and lofty throne, with the train of his garment filling the temple. Seraphim were stationed above; each of them had six wings: with two they covered their faces, with two they covered their feet, and with two they hovered. One cried out to the other:

"'Holy, holy, holy is the Lord of hosts! All the earth is filled with his glory!' At the sound of that cry, the frame of the door shook and the house was filled with smoke. Then I said, 'Woe is me, I am doomed! For I am a man of unclean lips, living among a people of unclean lips, and my eyes have seen the King, the Lord of hosts!' Then one of the seraphim flew to me, holding an ember which he had taken with tongs from the altar.

"He touched my mouth with it. 'See,' he said, 'now that this has touched your lips, your wickedness is removed, your sin purged.'

"Then I heard the voice of the Lord saying, 'Whom shall I send? Who will go for us?' 'Here I am,' I said, 'Send me!' And he replied: Go and say to this people:

"Listen carefully, but do not understand! Look intently, but do not perceive!

"Make the heart of this people sluggish, dull their ears and close their eyes; Lest they see with their eyes, and hear with their ears, and their heart understand, and they turn and be healed.

"'How long, O Lord?' I asked. And he replied:

"Until the cities are desolate, without inhabitants, Houses, without people, and the land is a desolate waste. Until the Lord sends the people far away, and great is the desolation in the midst of the land. If there remain a tenth part in it, then this in turn shall be laid waste; as with a terebinth or an oak whose trunk remains when its leaves have fallen. Holy offspring is the trunk." (Isaiah 6)

1. **Everybody Worships Something**

2. **Nothing but God Is Worthy of Our Worship**

    A. He's the supreme authority.

    Isaiah 46:9–10

    B. He should take our breath away.

    1 Chronicles 16:9

    C. Yet we want something else.

3. **Nothing Is Worth More Than Christ**

    John 12:43

Discussion Questions

1. Whether we're doing it consciously or not, we all place something or someone on the throne of our hearts, and we worship it with all we've got. What competes with God for that place of highest honor in your heart?

2. If we decide that we want God's glory more than our own, we'll have to make some hard choices. Which of the following examples of relinquishing human praise is hardest for you?

    ~We relinquish human praise when we call something absolute Truth that our culture says is backward and judgmental.

    ~We relinquish human praise when our highest priority in raising our children is for them to have a living, dynamic relationship- more important than education or success or sports.

    ~We relinquish human praise when we are willing to serve behind the scenes with no acknowledgement of our contribution.

3. In the talk, Lisa said, "Jesus offers you His cross... Each of our crosses is fashioned for us individually, by the one who knows exactly what will lead us safely to heaven." Do you ever wish you had a different cross to carry? Do you agree that God has fashioned each of our crosses individually, and that He knows just how much we can bear? Why or why not?

NOTES

Appendices

NOTES

Appendix 1
SAINT THÉRÈSE OF LISIEUX

Patron Saint of Walking with Purpose

Saint Thérèse of Lisieux was gifted with the ability to take the riches of our Catholic faith and explain them in a way that a child could imitate. The wisdom she gleaned from Scripture ignited a love in her heart for her Lord that was personal and transforming. The simplicity of the faith that she laid out in her writings is so completely Catholic that Pope Pius XII said, "She rediscovered the Gospel itself, the very heart of the Gospel."

Walking with Purpose is intended to be a means by which women can honestly share their spiritual struggles and embark on a journey that is refreshing to the soul. It was never intended to facilitate the deepest of intellectual study of Scripture. Instead, the focus has been to help women know Christ: to know His heart, to know His tenderness, to know His mercy, and to know His love. Our logo is a little flower, and that has meaning. When a woman begins to open her heart to God, it's like the opening of a little flower. It can easily be bruised or crushed, and it must be treated with the greatest of care. Our desire is to speak to women's hearts no matter where they are in life, baggage and all, and gently introduce truths that can change their lives.

Saint Thérèse of Lisieux, the little flower, called her doctrine "the little way of spiritual childhood," and it is based on complete and unshakable confidence in God's love for us. She was not introducing new truths. She spent countless hours reading Scripture and she shared what she found, emphasizing the importance of truths that had already been divinely revealed. We can learn so much from her:

> The good God would not inspire unattainable desires; I can, then, in spite of my littleness, aspire to sanctity. For me to become greater is impossible; I must put up with myself just as I am with all my imperfections. But I wish to find the way to go to Heaven by a very straight, short, completely new little way. We are in a century of inventions: now one does not even have to take the trouble to climb the steps of a stairway; in the homes of the rich, an elevator replaces them nicely. I, too, would like to find an elevator to lift me up to Jesus, for I am too little to climb the rough stairway of perfection. So I have looked in the books of the saints for a sign of the elevator I long for, and I have read these

words proceeding from the mouth of eternal Wisdom: "He that is a little one, let him turn to me" (Proverbs 9:16). So I came, knowing that I had found what I was seeking, and wanting to know, O my God, what You would do with the little one who would answer Your call, and this is what I found:

"As one whom the mother caresses, so will I comfort you. You shall be carried at the breasts and upon the knees they shall caress you" (Isaiah 66:12–13). Never have more tender words come to make my soul rejoice. **The elevator which must raise me to the heavens is Your arms, O Jesus!** For that I do not need to grow; on the contrary, I must necessarily remain small, become smaller and smaller. O my God, You have surpassed what I expected, and I want to sing Your mercies. (Saint Thérèse of the Infant Jesus, *Histoire d'une Ame: Manuscrits Autobiographiques* [Paris: Éditions du Seuil, 1998], 244.)

Appendix 2
SCRIPTURE MEMORY

"The tempter came and said to him, 'If you are the Son of God, command these stones to become loaves of bread.' But He answered, 'It is written: Man shall not live by bread alone, but by every word that proceeds from the mouth of God'" (Matthew 4:3-4).

Jesus was able to respond to Satan's temptations because He knew God's truth. When He was under fire, He didn't have time to go find wisdom for the moment. It had to already be in His head. He had memorized Scripture, and found those words to be His most effective weapon in warding off temptation.

Do you ever feel tempted to just give in? To take the easy way when you know the hard way is right? Does discouragement ever nip at your heels and take you to a place of darkness? If you memorize Scripture, the Holy Spirit will be able to bring God's truth to your mind just when you need to fight back.

Ephesians 6:17 describes Scripture as an offensive weapon ("the sword of the Spirit"). How does this work? When negative thoughts and lies run through our minds, we can take a Bible verse and use it as a weapon to kick out the lie and embrace the truth. Verses that speak of God's unconditional love and forgiveness and our new identity in Christ are especially powerful for this kind of battle. When we feel defeated and like we'll never change, when we falsely assume that God must be ready to give up on us, the Holy Spirit can remind us of 2 Corinthians 5:17: "If any one is in Christ, [she] is a new creation; the old has passed away, behold, the new has come."

That's not the only way memorized Scripture helps us. The Holy Spirit can bring one of the truths of the Bible to our mind just before we might make a wrong choice. It's like a little whisper reminding us of what we know is true, but there's power in it, because we know they are God's words. For example, in the midst of a conversation in which we aren't listening well, the Holy Spirit can bring to mind Proverbs 18:2: "A fool takes no pleasure in understanding, but only in expressing his opinion." This enables us to make a course correction immediately instead of looking back later with regret. As it says in Psalm 119:11, "I have laid up your word in my heart *that I might not sin against you*" (emphasis added).

You may think of memorizing Scripture as an activity for the über-religious, not for the average Christian. A blogger at She Reads Truth (shereadstruth.com) described it this way: "Recalling Scripture isn't for the overachievers; it's for the homesick." It's for those of us who know that earth isn't our home—heaven is. It's for those of us who don't want to be tossed all over the place by our emotions and instead long to be grounded in truth.

But how do we do it? Kids memorize things so easily, but our brains are full of so many other bits of information that we wonder if we're capable of doing it. Never fear. There are easy techniques that can help us to store away God's words in our minds and hearts. Pick a few that work for you! YOU CAN DO IT!

Beholding Your King **Memory Verse:**

"My God will fully supply whatever you need, in accord with his glorious riches in Christ Jesus" (Philippians 4:19).

1. **Learning Through Repetition**

    Every time you sit down to do your lesson, begin by reading the memory verse for *Beholding Your King*. The more you read it, the sooner it will be lodged in your memory. Be sure to read the reference as well. Don't skip that part—it comes in handy when you want to know where to find the verse in the Bible.

2. **Learning Visually**

    Write the memory verse lightly *in pencil* on a piece of paper. Read the entire verse, including the reference. Chose one word and erase it well. Reread the entire verse, including the reference. Choose another word, and erase it well. Reread the entire verse, including the reference. Repeat this process until the whole verse has been erased and you are reciting it from memory.

3. **Learning Electronically**

    Go to our website under Bible Studies and save the *Beholding Your King* Memory Verse Image to your phone's lock screen. Practice the verse every time you grab your phone.

4. **Learning by Writing It Down**

    Grab a piece of paper and write your verse down twenty times.

5. **Learning by Seeing It Everywhere**

    Display the gorgeous WWP memory verse card somewhere in your house. Recite the verse each time you pass by it. But don't stop there: Write your verse down on index cards and leave it in places you often linger—the bathroom mirror, the car dashboard, on the coffee pot, whatever works for you.

6. Learning Together

If you are doing this Walking with Purpose™ study in a small group, hold each other accountable and recite the memory verse together at the start and end of each lesson. If you are doing this study on your own, consider asking someone to hold you accountable by listening to you say your verse from memory each week.

[31] Full-Color Free Printables available at walkingwithpurpose.com/free-printables

NOTES

Appendix 3
HOW TO DO A VERSE STUDY

A verse study is an exciting Bible study tool that can help to bring the Scriptures to life! By reading, reflecting on, and committing a verse to memory, we open ourselves to the Holy Spirit, who reveals very personal applications of our Lord's words and actions to our daily lives.

Learning to do a verse study is not difficult, but it can be demanding. In this Walking with Purpose™ study, a Bible verse has been selected to reinforce a theme of each lesson. To do the verse study, read the verse and then follow these simple instructions. You'll be on your way to a deeper and more personal understanding of Scripture.

- **Read the verse and the paragraph before and after the verse.**

- **Write out the selected verse.**

- **Paraphrase.**
  Write the verse using your own words. What does the verse say?

- **Ask questions.**
  Write down any questions you have about the verse. What does it say that you don't understand?

- **Use cross-references.**
  Look up other Bible verses that help to shed light on what the selected verse means. A study Bible will often list cross-references in the margin or in the study notes. Another excellent resource is biblegateway.com. This website allows you to enter a specific Bible verse and it will provide many cross-references and additional insights into the passage of Scripture you selected. Record any insights you gain from the additional verses you are able to find.

- **Make a personal application.**
  What does the verse say to you personally? Is there a promise to claim? A warning to heed? An example to follow? Ask God to help you find something from the verse that you can apply to your life.

The recommended Bible translations for use in Walking with Purpose™ studies are: The New American Bible, which is the translation used in the United States for the readings at Mass; The Revised Standard Version, Catholic Edition; and The Jerusalem Bible.

A SAMPLE VERSE STUDY

1. **Verse:**
John 15:5
"I am the vine, you are the branches. He who abides in me, and I in him, he it is that bears much fruit, for apart from me you can do nothing."

2. **Paraphrase:**
Jesus is the vine, I am the branch. If I abide in Him, then I'll be fruitful, but if I try to do everything on my own, I'll fail at what matters most. I need Him.

3. **Questions:**
What does it mean to abide? How does Jesus abide in me? What kind of fruit is Jesus talking about?

4. **Cross-references:**
John 6:56
"He who eats my flesh and drinks my blood abides in me, and I in him." This verse brings to mind the Eucharist, and the importance of receiving Christ in the Eucharist as often as possible. This is a very important way to abide in Jesus.

John 15:7
"If you abide in me, and my words abide in you, ask whatever you will, and it shall be done for you." How can Jesus' words abide in me if I never read them? I need to read the Bible if I want to abide in Christ.

John 15:16
"You did not choose me, but I chose you and appointed you that you should go and bear fruit and that your fruit should abide; so that whatever you ask the Father in my name, he may give it to you." Not all fruit remains. Some is good only temporarily—on earth. I want my fruit to remain in eternity—to count in the long run.

Galatians 5:22–23

"The fruit of the Spirit is love, joy, peace, patience, kindness, goodness, faithfulness, gentleness, self-control." These are some of the fruits that will be seen if I abide in Christ.

5. **Personal Application:**
I will study my calendar this week, making note of where I spend my time. Is most of my time spent on things that will last for eternity (fruit that remains)? I'll reassess my priorities in light of what I find.

NOTES

Appendix 4
COVENANTS – GOD'S FAMILY BOND[32]

The Bible can be a confusing book. It contains a lot of different *stories* about a lot of different *people* doing a lot of different *things* at a lot of different *times*. It can be pretty hard to keep everything straight! One of the most helpful ways to understand the Bible is through the **covenants** that unite God to His people. God's covenants are the "line" that connects the dots of all the various biblical characters into a single, divine story.

A covenant is a sacred promise or contract between people. A covenant is real. Its ultimate source is God Himself. A covenant comes from God and directs us back to Him. A covenant—although similar in many ways—is much more than a mere contract. Confused? Keep reading.

A covenant, in its fundamental meaning, establishes a bond of sacred kinship. Hold up, what does that mean? Basically, it means that covenants make families. A covenant is a family bond. When you're in a covenantal relationship with another person you're *family*. One of the most common examples of a covenant relationship is marriage. As a covenant, marriage is such a powerful bond that it doesn't make two people business partners, colleagues, or even "buddies"—it makes them family. It makes them one.

"THE BIBLE IS REALLY THE STORY OF GOD DRAWING US INTO HIS COVENANT FAMILY."

This is why contracts are different than covenants. Contracts are temporary business agreements. ("I'll give you this for that.") Covenants are lasting family-ties. ("I will be yours and you will be mine.")

The Bible is really the story of God drawing us into His covenant family. The Bible records how God, out of Fatherly love, wants to make us His divinely adopted sons and daughters. This is the purpose of the Bible. In fact, this is God's secret motivation behind everything He does. What an incredible thing this is! God wants us to be a part of His family. He wants to be our perfect, loving Father. We are to be His children.

---

[32] "Covenants – God's Family Bond" (reprinted with permission) is from the preface to the Life Teen edition of the NAB Bible. If you'd like more clear, candid, and authentic explanations of Scripture, go to http://store.lifeteen.com/catholic-teen-youth-bible.aspx to purchase your own copy. This fabulous edition of the Bible contains 128 pages of supplemental material that's down to earth yet meaty.

God's covenant family is expanding throughout Sacred Scripture and, as it does, you'll notice several covenants at different points. There are six major covenants listed below and as you can see in this list, God also gave His people special covenant "signs." These signs are meant to help us remember God's undying love and faithfulness every time we see them. They are spiritual reminders that help us not to forget about God's love and mercy.

Covenant with **Adam** who is a *husband* in a *marriage*
Covenant with **Noah** who is the *father* of a *household*
Covenant with **Abraham** who is the *chief* of a *tribe*
Covenant with **Moses** who is the *judge* of the *nation* of Israel
Covenant with **David** who is the *king* of the *kingdom* of Israel
Covenant with **Jesus Christ** who is the *royal high priest* of the *Catholic Church*

Looking at Scripture through these covenants allows us to break the Old Testament down into more manageable, "bite-sized" and easier to understand chunks.

So let's look at these covenants a little deeper:

Adam and Eve
This first covenant was simply the sign of who God is, written into man and woman. God anoints marriage as the first sacred bond between man and woman. They are to give themselves as a gift to each other, and by doing this give life to the entire human race. This imitates the love of Christ for the Church (Ephesians 5:21–30), a self-giving love. In this covenant, mankind drops his end of the bargain by engaging in sin. The result of this failure is that only through the cross will man be redeemed, sanctified and made whole again. Adam and Eve have children and the world begins to be populated, but God's revelation of who He is must wait as humanity continues to choose—some for God, some against God. We see this reflected in the story of Adam and Eve's sons, Cain and Abel.

Noah and His Family
God continues by expanding our knowledge of who He is by revealing Himself to Noah and his family. Despite the fact that the majority of the human race had turned away from God's desire to be in union with them, God shows that He is not going to repair the rift with mankind by simply wiping them all out and starting over; God reveals that He is going to work with what we have. This promise to the family of Noah is kept on the part of God, but once again humanity struggles with its ability to follow its creator.

Abraham, Sarah and Their Tribe

In the deepest revelation of God up to this point, God tells Abraham that He is going to bless the earth through Abraham's descendants. They will honor his name and become a great nation. Abraham begins as the leader of a small tribe who, at times, finds following God to be difficult. All three of the great monotheistic religions that exist today (Judaism, Christianity and Islam) claim this faithful father as their starting point.

Moses and the Israelite Nation

As the Scriptures move forward we find that the descendants of Abraham are called Israelites, named after the grandson of Abraham. These descendants have migrated to Egypt and grown to such a number that the pharaoh has enslaved them, for fear that they would take over the country. God raises Moses up to lead the people out of Egypt into their own nation. He gives them His name (Exodus 3) and a Law to follow that will set them apart from the surrounding nations. The law is designed to make them ready to bring forth the Messiah. This law is a combination of the Ten Commandments and the other Laws of Moses that teach the people how to worship God in their new land, how to keep themselves holy and to grow in their knowledge of God.

David and the Israelite Kingdom

After the Israelites settle in the new land called Canaan, they are ruled for a period of time by spiritual rulers known as Judges. These rulers are anointed by God to keep the Jewish people, the Israelites, from falling too far away from God. In time, the Israelites demand a king and eventually the kingship comes to a man named David. David becomes the greatest leader in the history of Israel, bringing military victory as well as spiritual blessing. His story is not without its challenges, but unlike those before him, his repentance is sincere and humble Unfortunately, those kings that succeed David do not follow his spiritual example. The kingdom is divided in two and the people are sent into exile. Years later, one small group returns to build up Israel again. Their struggle for survival makes up the last 500 years of the Old Testament, reaching its climax when the Maccabees fight for independence from the oppressive Greeks. They achieve this unlikely military victory through total faith in God.

It is through these covenants that we see a people growing in knowledge of God into the type of people that will be ready to bring forth a savior *Christos* or "Christ," which is Greek for "Messiah."

Appendix 5
CONVERSION OF HEART

The Catholic faith is full of beautiful traditions, rituals, and sacraments. As powerful as they are, it is possible for them to become mere habits in our lives, instead of experiences that draw us close to the heart of Christ. In the words of Saint John Paul II, they can become acts of "hollow ritualism." We might receive our first Communion and the sacraments of reconciliation and confirmation, yet never experience the interior conversion that opens the heart to a personal relationship with God.

Pope Benedict XVI explained that the "door of faith" is opened at one's baptism, but we are called to open it again, walk through it, and rediscover and renew our relationship with Christ and His Church.[33]

So how do we do this? How do we walk through that door of faith so we can begin to experience the abundant life that God has planned for us?

GETTING PERSONAL

The word *conversion* means "the act of turning." This means that conversion involves a turning away from one thing and a turning toward another. When you haven't experienced conversion of heart, you are turned *toward* your own desires. You are the one in charge, and you do what you feel is right and best at any given moment. You may choose to do things that are very good for other people, but the distinction is that *you are choosing*. You are deciding. You are the one in control.

Imagine driving in a car. You are sitting in the driver's seat, and your hands are on the steering wheel. You've welcomed Jesus into the passenger's seat and have listened to His comments. But whether or not you follow His directions is really up to you. You may follow them or you may not, depending on what seems right to you.

When you experience interior conversion, you decide to turn, to get out of the driver's seat, move into the passenger's seat, and invite God to be the driver. Instead of seeing Him as an advice giver or someone nice to have around for the holidays, you give Him control of every aspect of your life.

More than likely, you don't find this easy to do. This is because of the universal

---

[33] Pope Benedict XVI, *Apostolic Letter: Porta Fidei*, for the Indiction of the Year of Faith, October 11, 2011.

struggle with pride. We want to be the ones in charge. We don't like to be in desperate need. We like to be the captains of our ships, charting our own courses. As William Ernest Henley wrote, "I am the master of my fate: I am the captain of my soul."

Conversion of heart isn't possible without humility. The first step is to recognize your desperate need of a savior. Romans 6:23 states that the "wages of sin is death." When you hear this, you might be tempted to justify your behavior or compare yourself with others. You might think to yourself, "I'm not a murderer. I'm not as bad as this or that person. If someone were to put my good deeds and bad deeds on a scale, my good ones would outweigh the bad. So surely I am good enough? Surely I don't deserve death!" When this is your line of thought, you are missing a very important truth: Just one sin is enough to separate you from a holy God. Just one sin is enough for you to deserve death. Even your best efforts to do good fall short of what God requires in order for you to spend eternity with Him. Isaiah 64:6 says, "all our righteous deeds are like a polluted garment." If you come to God thinking that you are going to be accepted by Him based on your "good conduct," He will point out that your righteousness is nothing compared to His infinite holiness.

Saint Thérèse of Lisieux understood this well, and wrote, "In the evening of my life I shall appear before You with empty hands, for I do not ask You to count my works. All our justices are stained in Your eyes. I want therefore to clothe myself in Your own justice and receive from Your love the eternal possession of Yourself."[34]

She recognized that her works, her best efforts, wouldn't be enough to earn salvation. Salvation cannot be earned. It's a free gift. Saint Thérèse accepted this gift, and said that if her justices or righteous deeds were stained, then she wanted to clothe herself in Christ's own justice. We see this described in 2 Corinthians 5:21: "For our sake he made him to be sin who knew no sin, so that in him we might become the righteousness of God."

How did God make Him who had no sin to be sin for you? This was foretold by the prophet Isaiah: "But he was wounded for our transgressions, he was bruised for our iniquities; upon him was the chastisement that made us whole, and with his stripes we are healed" (Isaiah 53:5).

Jesus accomplished this on the cross. Every sin committed, past, present, and future, was placed on Him. Now all the merits of Jesus can be yours. He wants to fill your empty hands with His own virtues.

---

[34] Saint Thérèse of Lisieux, "Act of Oblation to Merciful Love," June 9, 1895.

But first, you need to recognize, just as Saint Thérèse did, that you are little. You are weak. You fail. You need forgiveness. You need a savior.

When you come before God in prayer and acknowledge these truths, He looks at your heart. He sees your desire to trust Him, to please Him, to obey Him. He says to you, "My precious child, you don't have to pay for your sins. My Son, Jesus, has already done that for you. He suffered, so that you wouldn't have to. I want to experience a relationship of intimacy with you. I forgive you.[35] Jesus came to set you free.[36] When you open your heart to Me, you become a new creation![37] The old you has gone. The new you is here. If you will stay close to Me, and journey by My side, you will begin to experience a transformation that brings joy and freedom.[38] I've been waiting to pour My gifts into your soul. Beloved daughter of Mine, remain confident in Me. I am your loving Father. Crawl into My lap. Trust Me. Love Me. I will take care of everything."

This is conversion of heart. This act of faith lifts the veil from your eyes and launches you into the richest and most satisfying life. You don't have to be sitting in Church to do this. Don't let a minute pass before opening your heart to God and inviting Him to come dwell within you. Let Him sit in the driver's seat. Give Him the keys to your heart. Your life will never be the same again.

---

[35] "If we confess our sins, he is faithful and just, and will forgive our sins and cleanse us from all unrighteousness" (1 John 1:9).

[36] "So if the Son makes you free, you will be free indeed" (John 8:36).

[37] "Therefore, if any one is in Christ, he is a new creation; the old has passed away, behold, the new has come" (2 Corinthians 5:17).

[38] "I will sprinkle clean water upon you, and you shall be clean from all your uncleannesses, and from all your idols I will cleanse you. A new heart I will give you, and a new spirit I will put within you; and I will take out of your flesh the heart of stone and give you a heart of flesh" (Ezekiel 36:25–26).

NOTES

Appendix 6
LITANY OF PRAISE[39]

Praise You, Jesus, You are my Life, my Love.
Praise You, Jesus, You are the Name above all names.
Praise You, Jesus, You are Emmanuel, God is with us.
Praise You, Jesus, You are the King of Kings.
Praise You, Jesus, You are the King of creation.
Praise You, Jesus, You are the King of the universe.
Praise You, Jesus, You are the Lord of lords.
Praise You, Jesus, You are the Almighty.
Praise You, Jesus, You are the Christ.
Praise You, Jesus, You are the Lamb of God.
Praise You, Jesus, You are the Lion of Judah.
Praise You, Jesus, You are the Bright Morning Star.
Praise You, Jesus, You are our Champion and Shield.
Praise You, Jesus, You are our Strength and our Song.
Praise You, Jesus, You are the Way for our life.
Praise You, Jesus, You are the only Truth.
Praise You, Jesus, You are the Real Life.
Praise You, Jesus, You are the Wonderful Counselor.
Praise You, Jesus, You are the Prince of Peace.
Praise You, Jesus, You are the Light of the World.
Praise You, Jesus, You are the Living Word.
Praise You, Jesus, You are our Redeemer.
Praise You, Jesus, You are the Messiah.
Praise You, Jesus, You are the Anointed One.
Praise You, Jesus, You are the Holy One of Israel.
Praise You, Jesus, You are the Good Shepherd.
Praise You, Jesus, You are the Sheepgate.
Praise You, Jesus, You are the Lord of hosts.
Praise You, Jesus, You are the Rock of all ages.
Praise You, Jesus, You are my Hiding Place.
Praise You, Jesus, You are the Savior of the World.
Praise You, Jesus, You are the Strong Tower.
Praise You, Jesus, You are the Mountain of Refuge.
Praise You, Jesus, You are the Bread of Life.
Praise You, Jesus, You are the Font of all holiness.

---

[39] Linda Schubert, *Miracle Hour: A Method of Prayer That Will Change Your Life,* (Santa Clara, CA: Miracles of the Heart Ministries, 1991), 6–8. Reprinted with Permission. http://www.linda-schubert.com/.

Praise You, Jesus, You are the Living Water.
Praise You, Jesus, You are the True Vine.
Praise You, Jesus, You are my Spouse, my Maker.
Praise You, Jesus, You are our Fortress.
Praise You, Jesus, You are the Deliverer.
Praise You, Jesus, You are our Victory.
Praise You, Jesus, You are our Salvation.
Praise You, Jesus, You are our Righteousness.
Praise You, Jesus, You are our Wisdom.
Praise You, Jesus, You are our Sanctification.
Praise You, Jesus, You are our Justification.
Praise You, Jesus, You are the Door.
Praise You, Jesus, You are the great I AM.
Praise You, Jesus, You are the great High Priest.
Praise You, Jesus, You are the Cornerstone.
Praise You, Jesus, You are the Sure Foundation.
Praise You, Jesus, You are our Joy.
Praise You, Jesus, You are our Portion and Cup.
Praise You, Jesus, You are my Healing and Wholeness.
Praise You, Jesus, You are our Covenant.
Praise You, Jesus, You are the Promise of the Father.
Praise You, Jesus, You are the Everlasting One.
Praise You, Jesus, You are the Most High God.
Praise You, Jesus, You are the Lamb that was slain.
Praise You, Jesus, You are the Just Judge.
Praise You, Jesus, You are the Balm of Gilead.
Praise You, Jesus, You are the Mighty Warrior.
Praise You, Jesus, You are my Defense.
Praise You, Jesus, You are the Bridegroom.
Praise You, Jesus, You are my Patience.
Praise You, Jesus, You are the Solid Reality.
Praise You, Jesus, You are my Provider.
Praise You, Jesus, You are the Resurrection and Life.
Praise You, Jesus, You are the Alpha and the Omega.
Praise You, Jesus, You are the Beginning and the End.
Praise You, Jesus, You are all that I need.
Praise You, Jesus, You are all that I want.
Praise You, Jesus, You are worthy of all praise!

Answer Key

NOTES

Answer Key

Lesson 2, Day One
1. Samuel thought that God would choose Eliab because he *looked* like a king. God told Samuel not to judge by appearance or height, and reminded him that He sees things very differently than man does. While people look at the outward appearance, God looks at the heart.
2. David had a pure heart. In speaking of him, God said, "I have found in David, the son of Jesse, a man after my heart, who do all my will" (Acts 13:22). It was David's surrender to the will of God that set him apart. David was not perfect, but the desire of his heart was to please God.
3. In Isaiah 53:2–3, we read that Jesus didn't have a majestic bearing that attracted people to Him. People weren't drawn to Jesus because of His physical beauty. He was spurned and avoided by many. So what drew the multitudes to Jesus if it wasn't His appearance? It was His love and care for them. His authentic, unconditional love that saw deep into the hearts of people was absolutely irresistible to those who had eyes to see. But not everyone was looking at His heart. According to John 1:11, He came to His people, but they didn't accept Him. Many of the Jewish people were waiting for a political Messiah who would overthrow the Romans who were oppressing them. Jesus wasn't what they expected. They wanted the Messiah to deliver a political kingdom, not a spiritual one. His popularity with the masses only made the religious leaders jealous. They couldn't see why the whole world would go after someone who sat with the sinners and outcasts.
4. David was a shepherd. He was willing to do anything to protect his sheep—even risking his own life. He attacked and killed a lion and a bear in order to save the life of his sheep. Jesus is the Good Shepherd. He laid down His life for His sheep.
5. **2 Samuel 6:14–15, 20–22** David valued God's opinion more than any person's. He was happy to make a fool of himself for God, offering Him lavish praise publicly.
   Psalm 51:1–3, ESV David's response to his sin was heartfelt repentance. He didn't run away from God. He didn't isolate himself, with nothing but shame and self-pity for company. He threw himself at the feet of God, trusting in His character, in His mercy and forgiveness.
   1 Chronicles 29:11, 14 David was humble. He didn't take credit for his achievements. He recognized that all he had and all he was came from God. A heart like his recognizes one's smallness before God, but instead of this truth causing feelings of insignificance, it inspires us to rejoice over the truth that our great and majestic God chooses to love each of us personally.

Lesson 2, Day Two
1. Jonathan was next in line for the throne. Protecting David's life meant that he would be at David's mercy and would lose the right to be king. When Jonathan protected David, it showed that he had enormous trust in and respect for God's plan. If God wanted to anoint David as the king, then Jonathan didn't want to get in the way. Jonathan was placing his life in David's hands, because as long as Jonathan lived, even if David wore the crown, Jonathan could be considered a threat to the security of the throne. His actions proved that he truly wanted what was best for David and whatever was God's will.
2. Answers will vary.

3. Jesus' inner circle of friends included Peter, James, and John. Within that smaller group was greater intimacy and vulnerability.
4. David had many low points in his life. Being hunted down by Saul certainly was a terrifying experience. Heading into countless heated battles and losing his best friend were definitely traumatic events. But perhaps the lowest point for David came when his son Absalom turned against him and attempted to usurp the throne. The son he had loved showed what he truly felt about his father. It wasn't only Absalom who turned against him. One of David's trusted advisers, Ahithophel, went over to Absalom's side. David abandoned Jerusalem in grief and distress. He had no one to turn to but God. He called out to God in Psalm 3:1–4, "O Lord, how many are my foes! Many are rising against me; many saying of me, there is no help for him in God. But you, O Lord, are a shield about me, my glory, and the lifter of my head."

Jesus also experienced this lonely place of grief. When He was in the Garden of Gethsemane, wrestling with God's will, dreading the reality of the cross, He asked His closest friends to accompany Him, but they could only come so close. He advanced a little, and then fell prostrate in prayer.

When David and Jesus experienced these incredibly difficult circumstances, the one thing their friends could do was to pray. And even in those moments of loneliness and fear, Jesus and David were never alone. God was always present.

Lesson 2, Day Three
1. David tore his garments in grief. He mourned and wept and fasted until evening. He was irate that the messenger who brought news of Saul's death would have had so little respect for the Lord's anointed (Saul) to have felt the freedom to take his life. He felt so strongly about this that he had the man put to death. David had had two opportunities to kill Saul prior to this, and one could certainly have made the argument that doing so would have been self-defense. But David had so much respect for God and His anointed that he chose to trust God's timing and protection rather than take matters into his own hands.
2. He told the people not to receive news of Saul's death as good news. He referred to both Jonathan and Saul as beloved and dear, swifter than eagles, stronger than lions. He told the women of Israel to weep over Saul, reminding them of his good points. Saul had clothed them in scarlet and finery. He had made the Israelites prosperous. David wanted the people to remember Saul's good qualities. He went so far as to command that the eulogy, or lament, for Saul and Jonathan be taught to the people of Judah. He wasn't just saying these things. He genuinely wanted Saul to be remembered kindly.
3. We should forgive because we are commanded to. God doesn't make this an option in the life of a Christian. He does this so that we can live in freedom. It's incredibly hard to forgive. When we are struggling to obey God in this way, we need to remember that we didn't deserve forgiveness from Christ, but He generously forgave us. Jesus reminds us that we received His forgiveness freely, without deserving it, and now we are to freely give. The response to His forgiveness that He asks of us is laid out in Scripture: "Put on then, as God's chosen ones, holy and beloved, compassion, kindness, lowliness, meekness, and patience, forbearing one another and, if one has a complaint against another, forgiving each other; as the Lord has forgiven you, so you also must forgive"

(Colossians 3:12–13). "For if you forgive men their trespasses, your heavenly Father also will forgive you; but if you do not forgive men their trespasses, neither will your Father forgive your trespasses" (Matthew 6:14–15).
4. When Jesus was insulted and suffered, He didn't threaten. He didn't retaliate. He didn't harbor bitterness. He even went so far as to forgive His enemies as He suffered on the cross. He trusted that God would judge righteously. When we have suffered at the hands of someone, God asks that we forgive that person. He also promises that He will judge the situation fairly. When we forgive, we don't say that the way we were treated was good, right, or acceptable. We are simply handing over the right to be the judge and asking that God judge the situation.

Lesson 2, Day Four
1. The Ark of God was in a tent in Jerusalem. David felt horrible that he was living in a beautiful home while God's dwelling was so simple. Now that the kingdom was experiencing peace, King David wanted to turn his attention to building a beautiful house for the Lord. Initially, the prophet Nathan told David that it was a good idea. But that very night, God spoke to Nathan. He told him that in all the time that He had rescued the Israelites from slavery and brought them into the Promised Land, He had never dwelled in a house. And He'd never asked for one. As good a dream as David's was, God told him that he would not be the one to build Him a house. That job, or honor, was to be given to David's son.
2. God said that instead of David building Him a house, He would establish a house for David. This house wouldn't be like any other; it would be a royal dynasty, a lineage, a kingdom that would last forever.
3. God had promised in His covenant with David to make his dynasty stand forever. He had promised to establish David's throne through all ages. This promise depended not on the obedience of David's descendants, but on God's faithfulness. If the descendants ignored God's teaching, decrees, statutes, and commandments, they would be punished. But God promised that it would not cause Him to withdraw His mercy toward them. By God's holiness He swore that He would never lie to David. This meant that David's dynasty was to be as eternal as the moon and sky.
4. **Acts 2:25–31** David never stopped believing that God would fulfill His promise to set one of David's descendants on his throne, and he had prophesied in his writings in the Psalms that the Messiah would be eternal—that He would be resurrected from the dead.
Isaiah 9:6–7, ESV The Messiah would sit on David's throne, which means He would need to be a descendant of David. He would rule as a wonderful counselor, hero, everlasting father, and prince of peace.
1 Samuel 16:12; Micah 5:2–4, ESV David, son of Jesse of Bethlehem, was anointed king by Samuel, fulfilling the prophecy that the Messiah would be of royal descent from the city of Bethlehem. Bethlehem was known as the City of David because this is where he came from. The prophet Micah foretold that the Messiah would be born in Bethlehem.
5. **A.** When the chief priests and scribes were asked by King Herod where the Messiah was to be born, they were immediately able to answer, "In Bethlehem of Judea," because they knew what the prophet Micah had foretold.

B. Herod was troubled by these words because he was afraid of being overthrown. He knew he wasn't the rightful heir to the throne of David. He was hated by the Jews, and the possibility of a new, powerful leader being born—one so anticipated that magi from another land were coming to pay him homage—was both threatening and terrifying to Herod. In order to protect himself, he ordered that all baby boys under the age of two who lived in and near Bethlehem be massacred. These children are considered the first martyrs, and their deaths are commemorated each year on the Feast of the Innocents, December 28. Joseph was warned of Herod's plan in a dream, and was told to flee with Mary and Jesus to Egypt. He took them there and stayed until Herod was dead. This fulfilled an Old Testament prophecy about the Messiah foretold by the prophet Hosea: "[O]ut of Egypt I called my son" (Hosea 11:1).

Lesson 2, Day Five
1. Mary and Joseph were from Nazareth. Somehow, God needed to move Mary to Bethlehem so that the Messiah would be born there, in the City of David, as the prophecy had foretold. According to the Gospel of Luke, this was accomplished when Caesar Augustus decreed that a census was to be taken that required all people to return to their towns of origin to be counted. This required Mary and Joseph to travel to Bethlehem from Nazareth.
2. God is not like a human being. He will never speak falsely. When He speaks, He acts. If He decrees something, it will come to pass (Numbers 23:19). Titus 1:2 affirms that God does not lie. According to Hebrews 6:18, it is *impossible* for Him to lie. Because of this, we should be strongly encouraged to hold fast to the hope found in His promises.
3. Answers will vary.
4. All the promises made by God in both the Old and the New Testaments find their fulfillment, their yes, in Jesus Christ. As theologian John Piper wisely said, "Every sinner who comes to God in Christ, with all his needs, finds God coming to him in Christ, with all his promises. When a sinful person meets the holy God IN CHRIST, what he hears is YES. Do you love me? YES. Will you forgive me? YES. Will you accept me? YES. YES. Will you help me change? YES. Will you give me power to serve you? YES. Will you keep me? YES. Will you show me your glory? YES." [40]

Lesson 3, Day One
1. The love that the Shepherd has for His sheep is intensely personal. He doesn't just love His children as a group; He knows and loves each one individually.
2. **Luke 15:4–7** Our Good Shepherd cares about each of us, individually. He cares if we are lost or at home in the safety of His arms. When one of us is lost, He goes in search of us. He *pursues* us. When we "come home," when we turn to Him, He rejoices because we have been found. He is never indifferent to His sheep.

---

[40] John Piper, "All the Promises of God Are Yes in Christ," Desiring God, December 31, 1989, http://www.desiringgod.org/messages/all-the-promises-of-god-are-yes-in-christ.

John 10:11–15 Our Good Shepherd lays down His life for us. Unlike a hired man, who is not a shepherd and whose sheep are not his own, Jesus will walk right into danger to protect us. Why does He do this? Because He knows us and loves us.

3. When a shepherd would lie across the entrance to the sheep pen, any wild animal coming to destroy the sheep would have to deal with the shepherd first. Jesus protects us in that same way. He stepped in the way of our impending spiritual death, and fought that battle for us. He emerged victorious, able to offer us eternal life. His protection is offered to us, but we need to accept it.

4. He proved that His love is utterly selfless when He died on the cross in our place. When He guides us today, He doesn't guide us to do things that benefit Him but hurt us. He is *for us*. In contrast, the devil wants to see us destroyed. He leads us to do things that may feel good in the short term but in the long term are harmful, and the minute things heat up, he is gone. When Jesus leads us, He is bringing us to a place of safety. He promises that He will never leave us. When life gets difficult or scary, He is there, carrying us through. Jesus is also gentle. He doesn't burden us beyond our capabilities. He recognizes our weaknesses, and only expects of us what we are capable of. His very own Spirit, the Holy Spirit, is placed within us to help us to become holy. When we are feeling overwhelmed, or as if what He is asking of us is just too much, we are wise to check whether we are doing things because He has asked us to or because of something or someone else. When we are being "docile sheep" under the care of the Good Shepherd we are assured that "No temptation has overtaken you that is not common to man. God is faithful, and he will not let you be tempted beyond your strength, but with the temptation will also provide the way of escape, that you may be able to endure it" (1 Corinthians 10:13).

5. God never promises to provide us with everything that we *want*. He promises to provide everything that we *need*. What we need more than anything is Him. We need to spend eternity with Him. We need strength to live gracefully, regardless of our circumstances. It is possible to be materially poor but spiritually rich. You can live in a tiny space and still have largeness of soul. When God looks at each of His sheep, He determines just the right combination of success and failure, just the right amount of material possessions, and just the right balance of difficulty and joy. He mixes together a perfect formula for each one of us, and it's different for each. His greatest desire is to spend eternity with us, and He gives us just the right life to bring us there. We will never lack; we can always be content, if we will keep our eyes on what we truly need in this life in order to be well prepared for the next.

Lesson 3, Day Two

1. **Fear** and peace can't exist in the same heart, so when we're afraid, we find it hard to peacefully rest. The **hunger** that we experience isn't necessarily physical. We can hunger for purpose, love, appreciation, security, and countless other things. A classic stealer of inner rest is any kind of **friction** in relationships—friendships or family. Many of us can't sleep at night as we rehash conversations and struggle with hurt and frustration. The **pests** that swirl around us can be unpaid bills, task lists that are never completed, physical aches and pains, or worries over circumstances out of our control.

2. The help we receive from angels is mysterious, yet powerful (Psalm 34:8 and CCC 334). "Beside each believer stands an angel as protector and shepherd leading him to life" (CCC 336). Psalm 121 assures us that our guardian is the Lord. He promises to guard us from evil and to guard our souls. There is no moment when He is off duty. According to Psalm 121:4, the Lord neither slumbers nor sleeps. He never leaves us. He watches and protects us (and our loved ones) every second of every day.
3. We settle for food that satisfies temporarily—things that bring us pleasure in the short term but don't have true meaning or eternal value. We get busier and busier, and convince ourselves that we have no control over our circumstances. We feast on entertainment—the Internet, television, movies, shopping, anything to distract us from dealing with our hunger of soul. Self-sufficiency (rooted in pride), people pleasing, comfort seeking, and the desire for instant gratification all must be rooted out of our hearts in order for God to fill them in the way that truly satisfies.
4. We are to keep our eyes on the Good Shepherd, listening to His voice and following Him. This means we don't follow the crowd, or our family, or our friends. Sometimes following the Good Shepherd will create friction in our relationships. In times like that, we need to be comforted by the presence of our Good Shepherd, knowing that when we continue to follow Him in the face of ridicule, He sees our faithfulness. He knows what it costs us. It consoles Him deeply when He sees that we are willing to suffer rather than betray Him. Sometimes the friction we're experiencing isn't caused by our faithfulness to Christ. It can come from our own sin or be the result of someone else's selfishness. Either way, we can be comforted by the presence of the Good Shepherd. He sees. He sees through actions and words to the motives in the heart. This should lead us to a place of confession if the fault is ours, or release as we trust that the Good Shepherd is in a better position to judge than we are.
5. The Holy Spirit ministers to us by healing the wounds of our sin, and renews our hearts from within through spiritual renewal. He applies the healing balm of His presence to whatever is causing frustration or pain.

Lesson 3, Day Three
1. Hebrews 5:11–6:1 warns us against being lazy and sluggish in the spiritual life. Hearing God's truth should cause us to apply it in our lives. When we just listen but do nothing about it, we remain spiritually immature. God wants us to receive His truth and grace, apply it to our lives, and then go out and encourage others to do the same. When we remain in the same place, never progressing, someone has to continue feeding us the basics when we should be out teaching and encouraging someone else. This doesn't mean that every person has the gift of teaching and should be in a classroom or behind a pulpit. It does mean that we should all be progressing in the spiritual life in such a way that our words have authenticity. Our lives should show that what we believe makes a difference. When we are growing in spiritual maturity, God will provide us with teachable moments in which we can pass on what we are learning to those who are hungry for truth.
2. Following Christ means self-denial. This doesn't mean that we hate ourselves. It means we deny the tendency in every human heart to be self-centered. Instead of placing ourselves at the center, we place Christ at the center. Picking up our cross means that

Answer Key

when life gets difficult, which it inevitably will, we keep going. Instead of complaining or crumpling to the ground, we ask God for the grace and strength to endure and to continue on the path to heaven.
3. Jesus asks us to love one another. This isn't a fluffy, sentimental love. This is the love He exemplified when He died for us. It's a call to a radical level of self-giving for the sake of the other. We love whenever we do something for someone else that requires sacrifice on our part. The more we do this, the more we realize that "it is more blessed to give than to receive" (Acts 20:35). With each act of selfless love, we are stepping into greener pasture with the Lord.
4. Answers will vary.
5. We become a temple of the Holy Spirit through baptism. This gift of the Holy Spirit gives us power to live and act under the prompting of the Holy Spirit. The gift is given, and then God respects our freedom. It is up to us if we are going to cooperate with those promptings. When we ignore them, we quiet the voice of the Holy Spirit in our hearts. When layers of sin grow thick, we no longer feel the convicting of the Holy Spirit as we do when we are regularly confessing our sins. Acts 5:32 tells us that the Holy Spirit is given to those who obey Him. This means that it's as we step out and obey that the power of the Holy Spirit manifests in us. The Holy Spirit doesn't catapult us out of bed, against our will, so that we spend time in prayer. We have to obey and take the first step. He doesn't take over our will. Instead, He waits to be invited. He waits for us to ask Him for help.

Lesson 3, Day Four
1. Starting in verse 4, the psalmist (David) begins to address the shepherd directly. He switches from third-person pronouns (*he* and *his*) to the second-person pronoun *you*. This portion of the psalm is describing the period of the year when the sheep and the shepherd are completely alone.
2. **Deuteronomy 31:6** Answers will vary.
   Isaiah 41:10 Answers will vary.
   Matthew 28:20 Answers will vary.
   Hebrews 13:5–6 Answers will vary.
3. God does as He wills with the powers of heaven. No one can prevent Him from doing what He wants to do. His iron will and omnipotence (power over everything) protect us. Nothing happens that He has not allowed. Nothing. He is in control and all-powerful all the time. He is the supreme authority.
4. **Matthew 18:10 and Psalm 91:12** We all have a guardian angel who protects us. These angels look upon the face of God. We truly have no idea how many times they intervene in our lives, preventing us from "striking our feet against a stone" (Psalm 91:12). They support and guard us wherever we go. Hebrews 1:14 describes angels as "ministering spirits sent forth to serve, for the sake of those who are to obtain salvation."
   CCC 890 and 896 We are protected from false teaching through the magisterium, the teaching arm of the Church. The magisterium helps us to sort through the many possible interpretations of Scripture, guiding us to the right ones. We are also given our bishops as protectors. They act as our shepherds, and are to care for us as they would their own children.

Lesson 3, Day Five

1. **John 6:54** He provides us with His own body and blood in the Eucharist to strengthen, nourish, cleanse, and protect us.
   Jeremiah 15:16 When Christ was tempted, His defense was the Word of God. Each attack from the devil was met with a quote from the Old Testament that fought lies with truth. Our Good Shepherd offers us His words in Scripture. He wants us to devour them daily, knowing that they will be our joy and the happiness of our hearts.
2. He endured false accusations, the betrayal of a friend, the agony in the Garden of Gethsemane, the scourging, humiliation, being spit on and beaten, being ridiculed, the loneliness of being separated from His heavenly Father, the guilt and shame of all the sin of mankind, and the excruciating pain of the cross. He also experienced the loss of His splendor and position in heaven when He came to earth.
3. In the sacrament of baptism, the anointing with oil signifies cleansing and strength. In the sacrament of the anointing of the sick, it signifies healing and comfort. In confirmation and ordination, it is the sign of consecration.
4. In confirmation, the confirmand receives the mark, or seal, of the Holy Spirit with the anointing with oil. "This seal of the Holy Spirit marks our total belonging to Christ, our enrollment in his service for ever, as well as the promise of divine protection" (CCC 1296).
5. Answers will vary.

Lesson 4, Day One

1. Envy, a capital sin, is the sadness that comes from seeing another person's goods, accompanied by the desire to acquire them for oneself. It's saying (inwardly or out loud), "I want what you have, and if I could, I'd take it from you. I resent that things are going better for you than they are for me. I don't think it's fair." The Bible clearly states that we are not to envy. Envy is listed in 1 Peter 2:1 along with malice, deceit, insincerity, and slander, and we are told to get rid of it. All of these sins hurt our relationships with others and get in the way of our ability to love them.
2. **Verse 3**
   trust in the Lord and do good
   I will dwell in the land and live secure
   Verse 4
   find my delight in the Lord
   God will give me my heart's desire
3. He will make our righteousness shine like the dawn. This means that He will do a work within us that transforms us, making us the holy, strong, effective women He created us to be. He will make our justice like noonday. The strongest, brightest light will shine and God will work His justice. In the end, it will all be made right. Our God is a just God. If it seems like the people who are ignoring Him and His commandments are the ones who are getting ahead and having the nicer lives, be assured, vindication will come. Justice will triumph in the end. But we need to "[b]e still before the Lord, and wait patiently for him" (Psalm 37:7).
4. It was envy that caused the religious leaders to want Jesus dead. The Scribes and Pharisees should have loved Him—He was, after all, their long-awaited Messiah. But

envy got in the way and they had Him killed instead. They wanted what Jesus had: power and popularity with the people.

Lesson 4, Day Two
1. His enemies are saying bad things about him, whispering and gossiping about him. Even more hurtful is the lack of sincerity from a friend who visited, acting one way in person, but then speaking maliciously later. Even his trusted friend has betrayed him.
2. Jesus was betrayed by one of His disciples, Judas, and it led to His death. When Jesus indicated who would betray Him, the phrase "one who is dipping bread in the same dish with me" (Mark 14:20) was significant. In the east at the time of Christ, two people wouldn't eat out of the same dish unless there was a strong attachment between them.
3. Answers will vary.
4. Answers will vary.
5. When we second-guess God's motives when He gives something to us or withholds something from us, we are imagining the worst about Him. Instead of focusing on the times when He has proved faithful to us (even when we have been faithless), we dwell on the what-ifs. When we hesitate to trust Him, it causes Him pain. This is not how we want to be treated in friendship, so we should do our best not to treat God in this way. When we are in the midst of suffering, we should offer to God the same benefit of the doubt that we would give a girlfriend. In fact, we should offer Him far more, because in holding nothing back from us He has proved Himself to us beyond a doubt. He proved His love and trustworthiness through Jesus' suffering and death on the cross.

Lesson 4, Day Three
1. He turned *to* God, not *away* from Him. He focused on and appealed to God's character—His mercy, love, and compassion. This is how God had revealed Himself in Exodus 34:6–7: "The Lord, the Lord, a God merciful and gracious, slow to anger, and abounding in mercy and faithfulness, keeping merciful love for thousands, and forgiving iniquity and transgression and sin."
2. He asked for cleansing from his sin. God promises that He will always forgive our sins, but that doesn't mean that we don't have to ask. He forgives in response to our confession: "*If* we confess our sins, he is faithful and just, and will forgive our sins and cleanse us from all unrighteousness" (1 John 1:9; emphasis added).
3. In verse 3, David wrote, "For I know my transgressions, and my sin is ever before me." It was heavy on his heart. It continually pricked his conscience. Then in verse 6, he acknowledged that his sin was against God alone. But hadn't David also hurt people? Yes, but according to CCC 1850, "Sin is an offense against God." David recognized that his sin not only hurt the people in his path; its trajectory continued and wounded God Himself. We also see in verse 6 that he did not justify his actions. He didn't make excuses. He "owned his stuff," and acknowledged that God was without reproach in His judgment. God didn't owe David mercy. Then in verse 7, David said that he was born in guilt. He recognized that at no point was he ever without sin. In verse 8, he drew attention to the fact that God had secretly taught him wisdom. God had blessed David with a deep understanding of who He was. Theirs was an intimate relationship. God had given David wisdom and allowed him to experience closeness to Him. Perhaps this made

his sin even more mortifying to him. He knew better, yet even in the face of so much knowledge about God's goodness and what He expected of David, he ignored it and sinned.
4. David pleaded with God for renewal—for a fresh start. He wanted more than just forgiveness. He wanted to change. He wanted to be transformed. "Put a new and right spirit within me!" he cried. He recognized that this could only be accomplished through God's work within him. The good news is, there is nothing God would rather do. He loves to turn us around, renew our hearts, and set us back on the path of holiness.
5. We are promised in Romans 8:1 that "there is therefore now no condemnation for those who are in Christ Jesus." When we as God's beloved daughters feel the weight of condemnation, that is *not* coming from God. Condemnation comes when we look back at previously confessed sins and still feel guilty. By contrast, God *convicts* our hearts. Conviction occurs when God taps on our hearts and points out something new that we need to confess. We need to trust Christ's death on the cross as payment for our sins, instead of trusting our feelings. Even if we don't feel forgiven, that does not change the facts. We are forgiven because of Christ's blood, shed on the cross. How it must grieve God's heart when He knows what our forgiveness cost Christ—what it meant for Him to be able to offer us freedom and a fresh start—and we choose to stay in a place of bondage to our guilt. God wants us to come to the cross and leave our sins at the feet of Christ. He does not want us dragging our sins around as baggage that keeps us from living in freedom. We are to set our hearts at rest: "By this we shall . . . reassure our hearts . . . whenever our hearts condemn us; for God is greater than our hearts, and he knows everything" (1 John 3:19–20).

Lesson 4, Day Four
1. When he wrote that his flesh was failing, he was describing a physical struggle—perhaps feeling utterly worn out, depleted, unable to keep going. The phrase "my heart may fail" speaks of emotional despondency. It's a feeling of discouragement, of black hopelessness that can't see the point in pressing on anymore.
2. Answers will vary.
3. When we feel that we are sinking in a mess of undesirable emotions and circumstances, there is something solid that we can stand on. God is the rock of our hearts. When we feel weak, He provides strength within so that we can keep going. This makes all the difference. Our belief in God should prevent us from giving in. Our faith in Him empowers us to say, "I will not yield! I will continue to fight the good fight!"
4. Both the psalmist and Jesus looked ahead and found it hard to continue on the path marked out for them. Jesus was about to experience the worst suffering imaginable, and hoped that there might be an alternative, something that would still purchase our salvation but would allow Him to avoid such horrific pain. Surely Satan was there, tempting Jesus to question whether there was any point to what He was about to endure. But like the psalmist, Jesus held firm to faith. He did not yield to the temptation to give up. He pressed on. He resisted the temptation to waver from the Father's will in disbelief.
5. **Verse 37** Answers will vary.
   Verse 38 Answers will vary.

Verse 39 Answers will vary.
Verse 41 Answers will vary.
Verse 42 Answers will vary.

Lesson 4, Day Five
1. "Our mouth was filled with laughter, and our tongue with shouts of joy" (verse 2). "The Lord has done great things for us; we are glad" (verse 3). "May those who sow in tears reap with shouts of joy" (verse 5). "He that goes forth weeping . . . shall come home with shouts of joy!" (verse 6)
2. Answers will vary.
3. They had been brought out of captivity into freedom.
4. Jesus endured the cross because of the joy He knew He'd experience in the future. What future joy was this? When He experienced excruciating physical and spiritual pain, He knew that He was purchasing our redemption. That made the suffering worth it. He "dwelled in hope" because He knew that His Father would not "abandon [his] soul to Hades" or allow His body to "see corruption." He knew He would be resurrected from the dead, and that in conquering death, He'd be able to offer eternal life to us.
5. Jesus' joyful mission was to give liberty to captives and recovery of sight to the blind, and to let the oppressed go free. He was able to offer us liberty—to free us from captivity—by dying in our place, and conquering death. Death no longer has a hold on us. This is what allowed Saint Paul to write, "Death is swallowed up in victory. O death, where is your victory? O death, where is your sting?" (1 Corinthians 15:55).

Lesson 6, Day One
1. As seen in Lesson 7 (Moses) of *Beholding His Glory*, God delivered the Israelites from slavery in Egypt. When He promised this deliverance in Exodus 6:6, He said, "I will redeem you with an outstretched **arm** and with great acts of judgment." God spoke of His rescue of the Israelites in Deuteronomy 4:34-35: "Has God ever attempted to go and take a nation for himself from the midst of another nation, by trails, by signs, by wonders, and by war, by a mighty hand and an outstretched **arm**, and by great terrors, according to all that the LORD your God did for you in Egypt before your eyes? To you it was shown, that you might know that the LORD is God; there is no other besides him." God allowed them to see Him at work so that they would recognize that there is no God like our God, and respond to this reality with worship and faith. This belief in God's ability to do anything should have been passed from generation to generation. Not only should the Israelites have believed at the time of the miracles in Egypt, they should have still been believing at the time of Isaiah.
2. Isaiah's prophecy in Isaiah 53:1 was fulfilled when the Israelites didn't believe that Jesus was the Messiah, despite His miracles, wisdom, and unparalleled love.
3. To make an act of faith in Jesus as the promised Messiah required a mysterious death to self—a conversion. It required the religious authorities to let go of what they had expected the Messiah to be like, and to accept God's way of redeeming Israel. They wanted a rescue from a worldly king. God's plan flew in the face of human pride and the way they thought redemption should occur. This death to self was as hard then as it is today. In order for us to believe in Jesus, we, too, have to die to self. There may be other

ways in which we wish we could be redeemed. Perhaps we'd prefer that God put our good deeds and bad deeds on a scale, and if the good outweighed the bad, that would be enough to be redeemed. Perhaps we'd just like God to take a general look at our lives to see if we are basically nice people, and then consider that good enough. When God tells us that being redeemed means dying to self and relying only on the merits of Christ, purchased for us on the cross, many of us prefer a different plan. God's plan, while simple, requires all we are.

4. The imagery of a sapling growing up from a shoot in the parched earth is a picture of the Messiah, who was prophesied to be a shoot from the stump of Jesse (King David's father). Isaiah 11:1 is a prophecy regarding the rise of a new Davidic king. Isaiah 11:10 expands on that prophecy by describing that king's rule.
5. Jesus didn't come as a handsome king, winning the hearts of the people by His physical strength and power. He didn't draw people with a celebrity wow factor. The very people who should have celebrated His coming instead spurned, avoided, and rejected Him. The religious authorities and many others considered Jesus ordinary—certainly not worthy of throwing out old habits, expectations, and securities.

Lesson 6, Day Two
1. Answers will vary. The verses might be rewritten to say, "We bore our own pain and the sufferings that were due to us. We were pierced for our own sins, and crushed for our iniquity. We bore our own punishment. We all had gone astray like sheep, and so we carried our own guilt with us as a consequence." Thank God that life isn't fair.
2. "Bruised" (RSV translation) and "crushed" (NAB translation) are accurate descriptions of what Jesus experienced when He who had never sinned became sin for us. He carried all of mankind's sins—past, present, and future. The weight of guilt, intensity of pain, and distance from the Father produced an inward suffering beyond compare.
3. **A.** The whip used in the flogging of Jesus had lead balls and sheep bones tied into leather thongs. His flesh was pierced out of love for us. The lashing would have left raw stripes of exposed flesh across His body. The crown of thorns that pierced His brow was endured because He longed to see us healed. The nails that pierced His hands and feet released blood that purchased our salvation. The lance that pierced His side caused cleansing blood and water to flow out, all for our sake.
   B. When Jesus returns, "every eye will see Him, every one who pierced him." This might be a reference to the Roman soldiers who pierced His flesh at the crucifixion. But is this the only time that Christ has been pierced? Is He not wounded every time we sin? Could it be that this refers to our own eyes, beholding Christ in His glory? We, too, have pierced the heart of Christ.
4. According to these three verses, *all* have gone astray. We *all* have followed our own way. We *all* have sinned, and because of that, we are deprived of the glory of God. "If we say we have no sin, we deceive ourselves, and the truth is not in us" (1 John 1:8). While the mainstream culture decries social sin, there is a trend toward less focus on personal sin. Calling an individual's behavior "sin" is perceived as judgmental. In an atmosphere where all is relative, it's easy for us to justify personal sin if we can't see how it's hurting someone else, and if it feels good to us. Pope Benedict XVI addressed his concern over this cultural shift into moral relativism by saying, "It was maintained—even within the

realm of Catholic theology—that there is no such thing as evil in itself or good in itself. There is only a 'better than' and a 'worse than.' Nothing is good or bad in itself. Everything depends on the circumstances and on the end in view. Anything can be good or also bad, depending upon purposes and circumstances. Morality is replaced by a calculus of consequences, and in the process it ceases to exist."[41] That being said, perhaps the greater problem is the ability of each one of us to justify our own sinful actions. Short lines at the confessionals should cause us to wonder if we take enough time to reflect on our own sinfulness and need of a savior.
5. Jesus endured the physical and emotional pain of the crucifixion so that we could be whole—so that we could be healed.

Lesson 6, Day Three
1. 1) The suffering Servant submitted; 2) the suffering Servant didn't open His mouth—He was silent.
2. At every moment, Jesus was completely in control. No one took His life from Him—He laid it down on His own. He had the power to lay it down and the power to take it up (John 10:18). At any moment during His passion, He could have asked His Father to send Him more than twelve legions of angels to rescue Him. Jesus choose not to do this so that the Scriptures would be fulfilled in exactly the way the prophets had spoken (Matthew 26:53–54).
3. When Jesus was accused by false witnesses before the religious leaders, the high priest asked for His response. Jesus was silent. When Jesus was questioned by Pilate, the chief priests and elders testified against Him. Pilate looked to Jesus for a reaction, and was amazed when He said nothing. Herod was glad to see Jesus; he had been curious about Him and hoped that He would perform a miracle for him. He questioned Jesus at length, but Jesus didn't answer. He remained silent.
4. Answers will vary. Even when we are insulted and suffering, we aren't given carte blanche to respond sinfully. We aren't to insult someone back, or threaten. We're to respond with grace. The only way we can do this is to follow Christ's example, "trusting [ourselves] to him who judges justly" (1 Peter 2:23). When we respond with grace, we aren't saying that the behavior of the other person is OK. We're not saying that there aren't any consequences. But we are giving up the right to be the judge. We're handing ourselves over to God—who judges justly—and are allowing Him to mete out any necessary punishment.
5. Answers will vary.

Lesson 6, Day Four
1. "To bruise him" refers to Jesus' crucifixion. "Shall prolong his days" refers to Jesus' resurrection and eternal life. "He shall see his offspring" refers to all the people He will save from sin and death because of His substitutionary death.

---

[41] Pope Benedict XVI, "Address of His Holiness Benedict XVI on the Occasion of Christmas Greetings to the Roman Curia: *Sala Regia*, 20 December, 2010," Holy See, http://www.vatican.va/holy_father/benedict_xvi/speeches/2010/december/documents/hf_ben-xvi_spe_20101220_curia-auguri_en.html.

2. God can't just ignore sin. It dishonors His name. He can't act as if sin, which falls short of His glory, doesn't matter. God has said that "the wages of sin is death" (Romans 6:23). He can't go back on His word. That would be inconsistent with His character, His reputation, His name.
3. Christ's death on the cross shouts that sin (falling short of God's glory) has consequences. God never went back on His word, glossing over our sin, saying that the wages of sin *wasn't* death. A death was required. But it wasn't our death. When God allowed Jesus to die in our place, He showed the supreme value of His glory, and His limitless mercy and love for us. Jesus' willingness to die in our place also demonstrates to the world how much God's glory matters. When He suffered on the cross and gave up His life, He showed both His love for sinners and His deep desire to see God's holiness honored and satisfied.
4. Our sins were placed on Jesus, and He "[made] himself an offering for sin" (CCC 615). Just as the Israelites placed their hands on the lamb to be sacrificed for their sins, and the sins were transferred to the lamb, our sins were transferred to Jesus. Jesus' death for our sins atoned for our faults and satisfied God. Because of Jesus, we are considered righteous before God.
5. Once we were slaves to sin. Our own pleasures mastered us. Now that Christ has purchased our freedom, we have a new master. No longer slaves to sin, we're slaves to righteousness. Christ gives us the power to pursue holiness, but we sometimes do so in a halfhearted way. When we stop and think about what it cost Him to offer us freedom from slavery to sin, we can see how the only appropriate response from us is to love and obey God wholeheartedly.

Lesson 6, Day Five
1. The just One will justify the many and bear their iniquity.
2. Justification detaches us and purifies us from sin. The One who initiates this journey is God Himself, as it begins with His offer of forgiveness. Justification takes away our sins, and makes us holy. It renews us inwardly and gives us a fresh start.
3. To experience justification, we need to accept God's righteousness through faith in Jesus Christ. We must be baptized, as that is when justification is conferred. Baptism is the sacrament of faith.
4. We must believe with the heart in order to be justified—to be declared "not guilty." We often settle for intellectual agreement with what we hear or read, instead of taking the time to personalize those truths. We give intellectual assent but don't meditate on the greatness of God's love for us personally, and what our personal sins cost Christ. When we believe with the heart, we should experience a "radical reorientation of our whole life, a return, a conversion to God with all our heart, an end of sin, a turning away from evil, with repugnance toward the evil actions we have committed. At the same time it entails the desire and resolution to change one's life, with hope in God's mercy and trust in the help of his grace" (CCC 1431). This is a description of a radical life change that is deeply personal.
5. Answers will vary.

Answer Key

Lesson 7, Day One
1. God had brought them out of the land of Egypt, led them through the wilderness, and then brought them into the garden land (the Promised Land). They had responded by withdrawing from Him, going after emptiness, defiling the Promised Land, and turning God's heritage into an abomination. They went after useless idols, changing their glory for useless things. They turned away from God.
2. Answers will vary.
3. It's described as forsaking the living waters and instead digging cisterns that are broken and can't hold water. Instead of turning to broken cisterns, we should turn to Jesus, the living water. He offers us water (the revelation of who He is and the difference He makes), and if we'll embrace it, it will well up within us and give us eternal life.
4. **A.** Answers will vary.
   B. In order to avoid the path of compromise—trying to serve two masters—we need to have a wholehearted desire for God. He should be more important to us than anything else. The parable in Matthew describes a merchant looking for a pearl. When he finds that pearl, he deems it worthy of selling all he has in order to acquire it. His devotion and desire is single-minded and wholehearted. Loving God with this level of devotion will require letting go of other desires. We can't have it all. We must decide what has the greatest worth, and pursue it with all we've got. Anything that we love or desire more than God (think of your answer to 4A) can potentially lead us to make choices that compromise our love for Him.
5. Saint Paul considered all those things a loss when he compared them to knowing Christ. He considered them rubbish. Knowing Christ made him reassess the value of everything he had previously pursued. He discovered that true significance was found in Christ.

Lesson 7, Day Two
1. Jeremiah described the heart as tortuous, beyond remedy, and difficult to understand. The Hebrew word translated "tortuous" is *acob*, and means "crooked, deceitful, insidious."
2. **A.** Their hearts were "crooked"—inclined to evil. They knew what was right, but lacked the power to *do* what was right.
   B. The law was given so that the Israelites would recognize God and serve Him as the one living and true God. It was to help them see Him as "the provident Father and just judge," so that they'd "look for the promised Savior" (CCC62).
3. In Luke 6:45, Jesus said that the good man brings good things out of the good stored up in his heart, and the evil man brings evil things out of the evil stored up in his heart. Out of the overflow of the heart, the mouth speaks.
4. The heart is our "hidden center." Just as Jeremiah said, we can't really understand the heart of another person, and even our own heart can confuse us. Only God fully knows the human heart. This is the place where we make our decisions, choosing life or death. It's the inner place where we encounter God, the place of covenant, of commitment to a relationship with Him.
5. Conversion of heart requires humility. Our starting point must be our recognition that we need a Savior. If we choose instead to justify our behavior, or try to convince God

that our good deeds outweigh our bad deeds, we'll miss out on the salvation that is offered to us as a gift.

Lesson 7, Day Three
1. The New Covenant places God's laws within His people, writing it on their hearts. God promises to be their God, and that they will be His people. He promises to forgive iniquity and no longer remember their sin.
2. Jesus was the just shoot that sprang from David. He was David's descendant and successor, and did what was right and just. Because of Jesus, Judah and Jerusalem were saved. Because of Jesus, you and I are saved. The Lord is justice. There must be a punishment for sin. How incredible is our salvation that it would come through the Lord Himself taking the punishment that was due us.
3. The law would be written on the heart of Jesus. He would be born subject to the law. He would stand in the place of the people, and take on Himself "the curse of the law," which is the punishment due those who didn't abide by the law. The transgressions under the first covenant (disobedience of God's commands) were placed on Jesus, and He died to satisfy the requirement of justice.
4. We can become children of God. This has always been the Father's desire. He longs for intimacy of relationship with children who can "see what love the Father has given [them]" (1 John 3:1).
5. We receive power through the Holy Spirit.

Lesson 7, Day Four
1. **A.** He promised to sprinkle clean water on us and cleanse us of sin.
   B. According to CCC 1432, the human heart is heavy and hardened before God changes it. Our hearts are originally inclined away from God, not toward Him. So God woos us to Him, as seen in John 6:44: "No one can come to me unless the Father who sent me draws him." "Conversion [the process by which we receive a new heart] is first of all a work of the grace of God" (CCC 1432). God draws us to Him, and gives us the strength and cleansing needed for a fresh start. Our correct response should be an increased awareness of God's great love, which results in a horror of sin and fear of offending God. The more we focus on Christ's sacrifice for us on the cross and what that means for us personally, the more deeply our hearts will be changed.
2. When a woman has a new heart, the Holy Spirit is put within her so that she can live as a beloved daughter of God. Because of the Holy Spirit, she has the strength and power to obey, even when it's hard and requires sacrifice.
3. Water signifies the Holy Spirit's action in baptism. It's the sacramental sign of our new birth.
4. Answers will vary.

Lesson 7, Day Five
1. God said that He'd put breath into them.
2. The bones represented the whole house of Israel. The people were utterly without hope—expelled from the Promised Land, strangers in a land not their own. They had no power to get back all that they had lost. Yet God promised that He would cause sinews,

flesh, and skin to grow on the bones, and for breath to enter them. They would be given new life. God would take them from a place as hopeless as death and bring them back home. This vision began to be fulfilled when the Israelites, exiled in Babylon, were allowed to return to the Promised Land in 538 BC.

3. Because the Holy Spirit dwells in us, we have access to power, love, and self-control that goes far beyond our own resources. Are you afraid? God didn't give you a spirit of cowardice or fear. The Holy Spirit within you is a spirit of power, love, and self-control. Because of this, you can endure and overcome things you never thought possible. As Jesus said, "With men this is impossible, but with God all things are possible" (Matthew 19:26).

4. God raised Jesus, releasing Him from the throes of death. Death could not hold Him; the grave could not keep Him. It was utterly impossible for Jesus to be held by death.

Lesson 8, Day One

1. No one in heaven, on earth, or under the earth was worthy to open the scroll or to examine it. This truth is confirmed in Ecclesiastes 7:20: "Surely there is not a righteous man on earth who does good and never sins."

2. He is described as the lion of the tribe of Judah and the root of David. These are messianic titles for Jesus.

3. The lion of Judah was allowed to open the scroll because He triumphed over sin, death, principalities, and powers with His death and resurrection (Colossians 2:15). Only Jesus could have triumphed over sin and death. God required a perfect sacrifice—a person without sin—to satisfy His justice. No one else was worthy. Only Jesus was unblemished by sin—spotless and pure. He had to be a man to stand in our place. He had to be perfect to satisfy the requirements of a sacrifice. He had to be God to be powerful enough to rise from the dead. Only Jesus could be triumphant. Only Jesus was worthy.

4. **A.** One expects to see a powerful lion, because that's how He was described in Revelation 5:5. But He appeared instead as a slain lamb.
   B. When Abraham was asked to sacrifice his son Isaac, God told him to stop when his knife was poised in the air, and God Himself provided a ram to be sacrificed in Isaac's place. The lamb that was sacrificed at the Passover died in the place of the firstborn of the household. God commanded the Israelites to continue celebrating the Passover to remember the Exodus. In addition, sacrifices for the Israelites' sins were regularly made in the temple. The Israelites would take an unblemished lamb, place their hands upon it, and the sins of the man would be transferred to the animal, and the lamb would be killed in the man's place. All of this prefigured the ultimate sacrifice: Jesus, the unblemished Lamb of God, who was killed in our place.

5. We receive the power to live as God demands through the indwelling Holy Spirit. God never asks us to do anything that we are unequipped to do. The Holy Spirit is essential to living the victorious Christian life. Without it, we'll fail to be the women God has called us to be. It brings many spiritual gifts and fruits to our lives. Knowledge is one of the seven gifts of the Holy Spirit. "The fifth gift of the Holy Spirit, knowledge, is often confused with both wisdom and understanding. Like wisdom, knowledge is the perfection of faith, but whereas wisdom gives us the desire to judge all things according to the truths of the Catholic Faith, knowledge is the actual ability to do so. Like counsel,

it is aimed at our actions in this life. In a limited way, knowledge allows us to see the circumstances of our life the way that God sees them. Through this gift of the Holy Spirit, we can determine God's purpose for our lives and live accordingly."[42]

Lesson 8, Day Two
1. **A.** Their response was to fall down in worship before the Lamb.
   B. Answers will vary.
2. When we worship God or ask Him for what we need in prayer, our prayers rise like incense to the throne of God. Our prayers and petitions are ever before Him. They are a welcome aroma, a sweet fragrance before God.
3. At the Tower of Babel, the people were most concerned about making a name for themselves, not lifting up God's name. As a result, they were scattered over the whole earth and divided by language. The phrase "from every tribe and tongue and people and nation" (Revelation 5:9) is a picture of God unifying people throughout the world through the gift of redemption, and bringing them together as His family.
4. Jesus has made people from every tribe, tongue, and nation priests for God. This priesthood is different from the Old Testament priesthood. In the Old Testament, only the High Priest was allowed to be in God's presence in the Holy of Holies in the Temple. By contrast, Revelation reveals a kingdom of priests who are always in the presence of God.
5. **A.** All of our works, prayers, apostolic undertakings, family and married life, daily work and leisure, even our hardships become spiritual sacrifices acceptable to God. But this is on one condition: that we do it all through the strength of the Holy Spirit. This means that how we do these things really matters. Do we suffer patiently? Do we serve sweetly? Do we work with integrity? Do we love our family sacrificially? In addition, all of these things can be offered to God when we celebrate the Eucharist. Wherever we go, whatever we do, we can be worshipping God.
   B. We are the aroma of Christ in a world that desperately needs Him. We are to be the sweet fragrance of Christ wherever we go. He leads us in a triumphal procession throughout life, and as we go along, Jesus wants the people in our wake to be thinking, "I just smelled the freshness and aroma of Christ!" What lingers after you leave? The sweet fragrance of Christ?

Lesson 8, Day Three
1. Countless angels surrounded the Lamb, praising Him. The word *countless* in Greek is *muriades muriadon*, meaning "ten thousand times ten thousand," "innumerable," "multitude." This is a picture of an infinite number of angels worshipping Christ.
2. Isaiah had a vision of the Lord on His throne. He was surrounded by angelic beings saying, "Holy, holy, holy is the Lord of Hosts." We recite those very words as a way of praising God just before the consecration, when the bread and wine on the altar change into the body and blood of Jesus. Also called the Sanctus, this is a time when we

---
[42] Scott P. Richert, "The Seven Gifts of the Holy Spirit," May 11, 2016,
http://catholicism.about.com/od/beliefsteachings/tp/Gifts_of_the_Holy_Spirit.htm.

enthusiastically call out God's greatness. We can picture Him commanding a multitude of angels who live to bring Him honor.
3. They ascribed power, riches, wisdom, strength, honor, glory, and blessing to Christ.
4. All the power, glory, and honor that is due God the Father is also due Jesus. Jesus is more than a teacher or a good example to follow. He is fully God. "Throughout his public life, he demonstrated his divine sovereignty by works of power over nature, illnesses, demons, death and sin" (CCC 447).
5. Our knee should bend before Him, confessing Him as Lord. This means that we yield our personal freedom to Him, trusting that His power and strength will get us through anything He allows. We look at His sacrifice for us on the cross and are assured of His limitless love. This combination of an all-powerful and all-loving Savior strengthens our confidence and trust in Him. It isn't easy to surrender to Jesus. Most of us like to be as "in control" as possible. But the truth is, we can't control all things. Only God can. He's the one with the big picture, not us. In His infinite wisdom, He gives us just the right circumstances (a combination of blessings and challenges) to shape us into women of strength and dignity who are prepared to spend eternity in His presence.

Lesson 8, Day Four
1. **A.** Adam and Eve experienced total unity with God. They walked together in the garden. After they ate from the tree of the knowledge of good and evil, they were banished from the garden. Their intimacy with God was destroyed by sin.
   B. God told Moses to build a sanctuary. He dwelled in that sanctuary, or tabernacle, in the Ark of the Covenant.
   C. Solomon built the Temple, where the Israelites could come closer to God, pray, and offer sacrifices for their sins. God dwelt within the Ark of the Covenant in the Holy of Holies.
   D. Jesus, the Word, became flesh, and made His dwelling (or tabernacle) among us.
   E. Jesus promised that He would come to whomever loves Him and keeps His Word, and would make His dwelling with him. This promise was first fulfilled at Pentecost when the Holy Spirit descended. We are filled with the Holy Spirit; God now makes His dwelling within us.
   F. Christ comes into the depths of our souls through the Eucharist.
   G. He will dwell with us forever. He will always be with us.
2. God will wipe every tear from our eyes; there will be no more death, mourning, wailing, or pain.
3. Answers will vary.
4. Answers will vary.
5. This water is a symbol of eternal life.

Lesson 8, Day Five
1. Right now, our view of God is like a poor reflection in a mirror. But one day, we'll see Him face-to-face, and we will know Him *fully*. We'll know Him as intimately as He knows us. There will be no more barriers, and we'll have all of eternity to plumb the limitless depths of our Savior and God.

2. Heaven, the place where we will see God face-to-face in all His glory, is "beyond all understanding and description" (CCC 1027). Our eyes have never seen anything like it. We've never heard anything like what we'll hear there. Our hearts can't even imagine how amazing it will be. Jesus is there now, preparing it for us.
3. **Matthew 16:27** Jesus will come with His angels in the glory of his Father, and will repay each of us according to what we have done.
1 Corinthians 3:12–14 The foundation for our lives is Christ. How we build is referring to how we live. The quality of our "building" has to do with the motives behind our good works. Everything we do should be done to please God and to bring Him honor. We may do many good things with impure motives. When this is the case, the reward we've received on earth will be our only reward for that act. If we want our good works to survive and go with us to heaven, we'd be wise to check why we do what we do.
4. If we persevere, we will reign with Jesus in heaven.
5. If we remain steadfast under trial and are faithful to God, we will receive the crown of life.

Prayer Pages

NOTES

My Help, My Hope/Psalm 121

I lift my eyes to you
my help, my hope

the heavens (who could imagine?)
the earth (only our Lord)
the infinite starry spaces
the world's teeming breadth

All this. I lift my eyes
—upstart, delighted—
and I praise.

—Daniel Kerrigan, S.J.

Prayer Requests

Date:

Date:

Prayer Requests

Date:

Date:

Prayer Requests

Date:

Date:

Prayer Requests

Date:

Date:

Prayer Requests

Date:

Date:

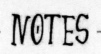

NOTES

NOTES

"For to the one who has, more will be given"
Matthew 13:12

The Journey Doesn't End Here
~ Christ's Love Is Endless ~

Walking with Purpose is more than a Bible study, it's a supportive community of women seeking lasting transformation of the heart. And you are invited.

Walking with Purpose believes that change happens in the hearts of women – and, by extension, in their families and beyond – through Bible study and community. We welcome all women, irrespective of faith background, age, or marital status.

Connect with us online for regular inspiration and to join the conversation. There you'll find insightful blog posts, videos, and free scripture printables.

For a daily dose of spiritual nourishment, join our community on Facebook, Twitter, Pinterest and Instagram.

And if you're so moved to start a Walking with Purpose study group at home or in your parish, take a look at our website for more information.

walkingwithpurpose.com

  NOTES

❋ DEEPEN YOUR FAITH ❋ OPEN YOUR ARMS ❋
❋ BROADEN YOUR CIRCLE ❋

When your heart opens, and your love for Christ deepens, you may be moved to bring Walking With Purpose to your friends or parish. It's rewarding experience for many women who, in doing so, learn to rely on God's grace while serving Him.

If leading a group seems like a leap of faith, consider that you already have all the skills you need to share the Lord's Word:

- Personal commitment to Christ
- Desire to share the love of Christ
- Belief in the power of authentic, transparent community

The Walking With Purpose community supports you with:

- Training
- Mentoring
- Bible study materials
- Promotional materials

Few things stretch and grow our faith like stepping out of our comfort zone and asking God to work through us. Say YES, soon you'll see the mysterious and unpredictable ways He works through imperfect women devoted to Him.

Remember that if you humbly offer Him what you can, He promises to do the rest.

"See to it that no one misses the grace of God" Hebrews 12:15

**Learn more about bringing Walking with Purpose to your parish.
Visit us at walkingwithpurpose.com**

walking with purpose

 NOTES

Walking with Purpose Devotionals

Daily affirmations of God's love

Rest: 31 Days of Peace

- A beautiful, hardcover, pocket-sized devotional to take wherever you go.
- 31 Scripture-based meditations that you can read (and re-read) daily.
- Become saturated with the truth that you are seen, known, and loved by a God who gave everything for you!

Be Still: A Daily Devotional to Quiet Your Heart

- Grow closer to the Lord each day of the year with our 365-day devotional.
- This beautifully designed hardcover devotional collection will renew your mind and help you look at things from God's perspective.
- Apply what you read in *Be Still*, and you'll make significant progress in your spiritual life!

shop.walkingwithpurpose.com

walking with purpose
SO MUCH MORE THAN A BIBLE STUDY

NOTES

Journal Your Prayers & Grow Closer to God

The Walking with Purpose *Praying from the Heart: Guided Journal* is a beautiful, comprehensive prayer journal that provides a private space to share your thoughts and feelings with the Lord.

Journaling your prayers lets you express a greater depth of intimacy toward God, and it will help you cultivate the practice of gratitude. Journaling will motivate you to pray regularly, too!

Praying from the Heart lays flat for easy writing, and is fashioned after the way that author Lisa Brenninkmeyer journals her own prayers. You'll love the heavyweight paper, luxurious leatherette cover, and many other special details.

shop.walkingwithpurpose.com

NOTES

Walking with Purpose
Seven Priorities that Make Life Work

Does your life feel out of control? Do you feel that you are doing so many things that you are doing none of them well? Did you know that Lisa Brenninkmeyer wrote a book to help you uncover the key to living a busy life with inner calm?

With humor and wisdom, Lisa will help you:

- Stop striving and rest in God's unconditional love
- Experience new hope in your marriage
- Reach your child's heart
- Create clarity in a cluttered home
- Find friendships that go below the surface and satisfy
- Discover your passion and purpose

Study Guide also Available

The book, *Walking with Purpose: Seven Priorities that Make Life Work,* and the accompanying Discussion Guide make up a 6-week study you can do on your own or with a group of friends.

Get your copy of Lisa's book,
Walking with Purpose: Seven Priorities that Make Life Work,
at shop.walkingwithpurpose.com

walking with purpose

 NOTES

Walking with Purpose™ Young Adult Bible Studies

Deepen Your Relationship with Christ

Catholic Bible Studies for Young Women

- Meeting young women where they are and pointing them to a life of freedom in Christ

- Based on our popular Bible studies for adult women and written especially for women in their late teens and twenties

- Each study guide contains five or six lessons to help apply Scripture to your daily life

- Great for personal meditation and group discussion

- Sold separately and in three-book sets: shop.walkingwithpurpose.com

Find great resources and tools to strengthen your Bible study experience!

walkingwithpurpose.com/young-adults

walking with purpose

NOTES

blaze for Tween/Teen Girls!

Do you want to help girls grow in confidence, faith and kindness?

The Lord is calling for women like you to speak truth into the hearts of young girls – girls who can be easily confused about their true worth and beauty.

BLAZE is the Walking with Purpose ministry designed especially for tween/teen girls. It makes the wisdom of the Bible relevant to the challenges girls face today, and teaches them to recognize the difference between the loving voice of their heavenly Father and the voices that tell them they aren't good enough.

You can be a positive influence on the girls you know by starting a BLAZE program for any number of girls in your parish, school or home (or use one-on-one)!

The 20-week **BLAZE Core Program** includes a Leader's Guide and fun BLAZE kits. Each kit contains a pack of Truth vs. Lie cards, materials for icebreaker activities, take-home gifts and the BLAZE Prayer Journal.

You might also like **Between You and Me**, a 40-day conversation guide for mothers and daughters to read together. The daily reflection, journaling opportunities, discussion questions, and prayer prompts will help take your relationship to a new level of honesty and intimacy.

Discovering My Purpose is a six-lesson Bible study designed to open girls' eyes to their unique purpose, gifts, and God's love. It includes the **BLAZE Spiritual Gifts Inventory**, a fabulous tool to help girls discern where God is calling them to be world-changers.

Learn more at walkingwithpurpose.com/BLAZE

"BE WHO GOD MEANT YOU TO BE AND YOU WILL SET THE WORLD ON FIRE."
SAINT CATHERINE OF SIENA

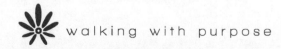

 NOTES

FEARLESS & FREE
EXPERIENCING HEALING AND WHOLENESS IN CHRIST

Fear is a powerful emotion, and part of the human condition. Life isn't easy. But we were never meant to go it alone. God has wired us for connection – to Him.

Do you long to be grounded in a love that will never fail you?

Fearless and Free is for any woman confronting the reality of her fears. When suffering slams into you and leaves you reeling, or you feel great one day, and down on the mat the next, turn to this Scripture study.

Do you long for healing and wholeness? Would you like to be grounded in a love that will never fail?

In these six compassionate lessons, you'll learn to:

- **WAKEN** to the reality of who you are in Christ,

- **WRESTLE** with the battle in your mind, and conquer the enemy who seeks to steal your true identity.

- Be strengthened as a **WARRIOR** to reclaim your footing and move forward in life.

Fearless and Free is not about surviving; it's about flourishing in Christ's love, the One who truly loves you completely and without end.

Learn more about *Fearless and Free* at walkingwithpurpose.com

The guided tour of God's love begins here.

Opening Your Heart: The Starting Point begins a woman's exploration of her Catholic faith and enhances her relationship with Jesus Christ. This Bible study is designed to inspire thoughtful consideration of the fundamental questions of living a life in the Lord. More than anything, it's a weekly practice of opening your heart to the only One who can heal and transform lives.

Explore these topics and more:

- What is the role of the Holy Spirit in my life?
- What does the Eucharist have to do with my friendship with Christ?
- What are the limits of Christ's forgiveness?
- Why and how should I pray?
- What is the purpose of suffering?
- What challenges will I face in my efforts to follow Jesus more closely?
- How can fear be overcome?

A companion video series complements this journey with practical insights and spiritual support.

Opening Your Heart is a foundational 22-lesson Bible study that serves any woman who seeks to grow closer to God. It's an ideal starting point for women who are new to Walking with Purpose and those with prior practice in Bible study, too.

To share Walking with Purpose with the women in your parish, contact us at walkingwithpurpose.com/contact-us.

walkingwithpurpose.com

walking with purpose

Transformative Catholic Bible Studies

Walking with Purpose Bible studies are created to help women deepen their personal relationship with Christ. Each study includes many lessons that explore core themes and challenges of modern life through the ancient wisdom of the Bible and the Catholic Church.

Opening Your Heart
A thoughtful consideration of the fundamental questions of faith – from why and how to pray to the role of the Holy Spirit in our lives and the purpose of suffering.

Living In the Father's Love
Gain a deeper understanding of how God's unconditional love transforms your relationship with others, with yourself, and most dearly, with Him.

Keeping In Balance
Discover how the wisdom of the Old and New Testaments can help you live a blessed lifestyle of calm, health, and holiness.

Touching the Divine
These thoughtful lessons draw you closer to Jesus and deepen your faith, trust, and understanding of what it means to be God's beloved daughter.

Discovering Our Dignity
Modern-day insight directly from women of the Bible presented as a tender, honest, and loving conversation—woman to woman.

Beholding His Glory
Old Testament Scripture leads us directly to our Redeemer, Jesus Christ. Page after page, God's awe-inspiring majesty is a treasure to behold.

Beholding Your King
This study of King David and several Old Testament prophets offers a fresh perspective of how all Scripture points to the glorious coming of Christ.

Grounded In Hope
Anchor yourself in the truth found in the New Testament book of Hebrews, and gain practical insight to help you run your race with perseverance.

Fearless and Free
With an emphasis on healing and wholeness, this study provides a firm foundation to stand on, no matter what life throws our way.

Reclaiming Friendship
Let God reshape how you see and experience intentional relationships, deal with your past friendship wounds, and become a woman who is capable of the lifelong bond of true friendship.

Ordering Your Priorities
An immensely practical study that will help you put the most important things first. Discover not only what matters most in life, but also how to prioritize those things!

Choose your next Bible study at shop.walkingwithpurpose.com

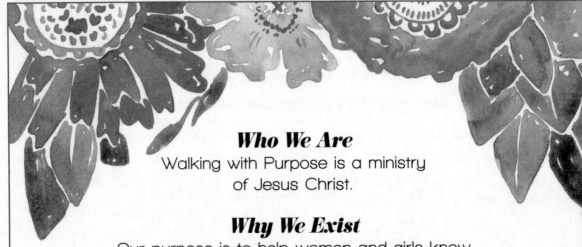

Who We Are
Walking with Purpose is a ministry
of Jesus Christ.

Why We Exist
Our purpose is to help women and girls know
Jesus Christ personally by making Scripture and the
teachings of the Catholic Church relevant and applicable.

Our Mission
Our mission is to help every Catholic woman and girl in
America encounter Jesus Christ through our Bible studies.

Our Vision
Our vision for the future is that, as more Catholic
women deepen their relationships with Jesus Christ,
eternity-changing transformation will take place in their
hearts – and, by extension – in their families, in their
communities, and ultimately, in our nation.

walking with purpose
SO MUCH MORE THAN A BIBLE STUDY

You can support our mission through a tax-deductible gift.
Learn more at walkingwithpurpose.com/donate